The
Lower American River
PREHISTORY TO PARKWAY

The Lower American River
PREHISTORY TO PARKWAY

Original Edition Edited By
Lucinda Woodward and Jesse M. Smith
April 1977

❧

Revised and Updated for the
American River Natural History Association
By William C. Dillinger
April 1991

❧

Updated and Expanded Edition
Edited by Peter J. Hayes *Peter J. Hayes*

Contributing Writers:
William C. Dillinger, Ed Littrell, Felix Smith
May 2005

American River Natural History Association

Copyright© 2005 by the American River Natural History Association

Published 1991 under the title
A History of the Lower American River

1st edition published 1977

2nd edition published 1991

Portions of information in Lower American River: Prehistory to Parkway may
be reproduced for educational purposes if credit is given to the source. Please
write for permission.

ISBN 1-887815-13-9

Front cover drawing courtesy of Sacramento City Archives and Collections
Back cover photo by Tom Myers

Book Production & Design: Mary L Chapeau
Typesetting: Kathie Nute
Cover Design: Molly Keller and Mary L. Chapeau
Map Illustration: Molly Keller
Printed In the United States: WW Hobbs Printing Ltd
Indexing by Brackney Indexing Service, Nevada City, CA

American River Natural History Association
P.O. Box 241
Carmichael, CA 95609 - 0241
(916) 489-4918
www.arnha.org

Dedication

Dedicated to all
who love and protect the river and parkway

Acknowledgements

1977 Edition

The first edition of *A History of the Lower American River* was produced in three manuscript copies. Subsequently, the Sacramento County Department of Parks and Recreation produced more than 100 copies of Volume One. These copies were distributed by Effie Yeaw and the Parks Department.

This 1977 project came as a result of a grant to Sacramento County by the Natomas Company for the research and document preparation. The County contracted with the Museum and History Division of the City of Sacramento to do the project. The research team that assembled the research document consisted of: Sannie Palumbo, Steve Helmich, Cece Martin, Janeann Porter, Jesse Smith and Lucinda Woodward. The "Prehistory" section was prepared by Sannie Palumbo. The team worked under the supervision of James Henley, who served as the project director. Lucinda Woodward and Jesse Smith revised and edited the first edition.

The project was conceived as a vision of Dante P. Lembi with the Natomas Company. Lembi worked for many years with the company records and shepherded many transactions of company land to Sacramento County for the American River Parkway. He understood the great importance of the American River and was dedicated to getting its history recorded. Dante Lembi, with the support of the Chairman of the Board of Directors of the Natomas Company, Chandler Ide, initiated the company's commitment to this project. The Natomas Company acknowledged Lembi's contributions by funding a park in Folsom in his memory.

— James Henley, Project Director, 1977 Edition

1991 Edition

The original 1977 edition of this book was essentially a research document published in a limited quantity for academic use. The material has proven of such interest, however, that the few dog-eared copies have become dearly treasured, and it has even circulated quite extensively in xerox form.

As a result, the American River Natural History Association requested and was granted a Civic and Cultural History Award from the Sacramento County Board of Supervisors to reissue the book in conjunction with an exhibit on the history of the lower American River at the Effie Yeaw Nature Center in May 1991.

It was ARNHA's decision that for broader public uses the book should be redone in a more "popular style," suitable for the general reader, as well as for background material for schools. The current editor has, therefore, undertaken to revise and largely rewrite the original version in ARNHA's behalf.

An introduction has been added to show how the different chapters tie together, and to try to convey an understanding of overall significance of the American River to the history of Sacramento and the West. The chapter on the Parkway has been greatly expanded, and the section on fisheries made into a separate chapter. All chapters have been updated, and some new material added where it seemed appropriate. Current issues affecting the river have also been discussed. Conversely, some technical material has been dropped — the extensive footnotes, a detailed listing of archeological sites, and some specialized items in the bibliography.

The volume remains based, however, on the excellent research done by the original team, with only an occasional amendment where it seemed desirable to try to clarify unclear spots in text or references, or to bring in information uncovered since the original work was done.

Special thanks are again due to James Henley of the History and Science Division, City of

Sacramento, and to Lucinda Woodward, one of the original editors, for reviewing the revised text. Thanks are also due to Carol Doersch of ARNHA for assistance in editing and revising the text; to Katy Harrington for transcribing and proofing the manuscript; to Diane Wysong from the History and Science Division for design, layout, and typesetting; and to Charlene Gilbert, the Archivist at the Sacramento Archives and Museum Collection Center, History and Science Division, for research assistance and locating the illustrations for this edition; and to the printer, River City Lithography.

The section on the American River Parkway was revised and updated by Jo Smith, a long-time proponent of the Parkway. Jo also revised and updated the section on the River's Fisheries, with the assistance of Editor William Dillinger, a current member of the SARA Board of Directors. The centerfold map was prepared by Art Bruer of the ARNHA Board of Directors, with the assistance of the editor and board member Robin Donnelly.

— William Dillinger, Editor, 1991 Edition

2005 Edition

This is the third edition of a volume that was originally edited by Lucinda Woodward and Jesse Smith in a team project under the supervision of James Henley, manager of the Sacramento Archives and Museum Collection Center. It was published in 1977 by the Sacramento Museum and History Commission and the Sacramento County Department of Parks and Recreation. In 1991, a revised and updated edition edited by William C. Dillinger was published by the American River Natural History Association (ARNHA). This 2005 edition, building on the earlier work and updated, is edited by Peter J. Hayes and again published by ARNHA. Ed Littrell of ARNHA contributed a new Fisheries chapter, William C. Dillinger expanded the Transportation chapter, and Felix Smith of the Save the American River Association updated the river's "water wars."

Georgia Jones of the ARNHA Publications Committee gave production and editorial assistance beyond measure. Artist Molly Keller of the committee donated her talents to updating the covers and history map. Committee members Peggy Kennedy, Betty Cooper, Claudia Hulbe, and Ann Doersch made key contributions. ARNHA Past President Greg Voelm shared valuable research. Save the American River Association members Jim Jones, Frank Cirill, Alan Wade, Jack Sohl and Wanda Denson contributed their hard-won expertise. James Henley and Lucinda Woodward provided generous support. Melinda Peak of Peak & Associates, Inc., Archeology Consultants, and Steve Beck, Sutter's Fort Historical Park archivist, reviewed the 1st chapter (First People) and made constructive suggestions.

Also, thanks to so many others who helped, including County Supervisor Illa Collin, Director Ron Suter and Deputy Director Gary Kukkola of the Sacramento County Regional Parks and Recreation Department; Gene Andal, former County Parks director; Dave Lydick, County Park Rangers manager; Kim Tremaine, Tremaine & Associates, archaeologists; Marilee Flannery, Effie Yeaw Nature Center director; archivist Patricia Johnson, illustration scanner/editor George Wilson, and administrative analyst Kristin Elder of the Sacramento Archives and Museum Collection Center; Ruth Ellis of the Sacramento Public Library Central Branch's Sacramento Room; William Holden, author of "Sacramento: Excursions into its History and Natural World;" Pete Ghelfi of the Sacramento Area Flood Control Agency; Chris Bowman, Sacramento Bee; Tracy Martin Shearer, Fair Oaks Bluffs preservationist; Merick Chaffee, retired, California State Parks; Charley Willard, California State Parks; Elmer Aldrich, retired, California State Parks; Amy Whitlach and Jill Stockinger of the Carmichael Library; Dan Lombard, Review Publishing Co.; Karen Niiya of the State Central Valley Regional Water Quality Control Board; and Dave Norris of the Sacramento County Department of Economic Development and Intergovernmental Affairs. Of course, any errors or inadequacies in this edition are my own.

— Peter J. Hayes, Editor, 2005 Edition

Table Of Contents

— The —
Lower American River
PREHISTORY TO PARKWAY

Introduction

Sacramento exists because of the American River.

For John Sutter, searching for high ground and a safe landing place, chose this spot on the south bank of the American River, just above its confluence with the more unruly Sacramento, to establish the initial outpost of New Helvetia, his dreamed-of inland empire.

He picked this place because it gave him easy access to the fertile lands of the flood plain, and provided an easy route, when most transport was by water, to the San Francisco Bay area, the nearest market for his produce and closest source for needed manufactured goods.

An added boon was the river's potential as an access to the timber and minerals of nearby foothills, and as a route for overland travel across the Sierra to his fort. It could also provide power for the lumber and flour mills he hoped to build.

In pre-settlement days, the American River regularly flooded much of what is now the City of Sacramento, bringing fertility to the land but creating what seemed in prospective settlers' eyes "an uninhabitable malarial swamp."

Many a dream like Sutter's lies buried under dry grass and brush, but the good Captain chose well. His wheat fields and cattle ranges did grow into a vast agricultural empire after he passed from the scene. The natural route over the Sierra and down through the American River watershed brought more and more emigrants to his settlement, which became the place of destination for the overland trail to California. His temporary landing on the Sacramento became a major river port and a rail and wagon road hub serving the hundreds of mining towns and camps that sprang up with the Gold Rush. And these facilities continued to serve when the economies of the foothill settlement turned to vineyards and orchards and cattle.

Already a transportation center, Sacramento was a logical choice as the western terminus of the first transcontinental railroad. Meanwhile, it developed as a commercial and manufacturing center in its own right. Gold and agriculture remained major attractions to the area, as placer mining in the streams shifted to hard-rock mining, hydraulic mining, and finally dredging, and the lure of fertile lands and sunshine brought thousands of hopeful new settlers to agricultural "colonies" optimistically named "Citrus Heights," and "Orange Vale" and the like.

Through all the years, it was the American River that bound everything together. Its waters irrigated the land. They powered sawmills and grist or flour mills. While the river was never navigable to any extent beyond Brighton, near the present-day California State University, Sacramento (CSUS), campus, the canyons and ridges formed by the river and its tributaries developed into the major travel routes through the foothills and on to the East.

The waters of the American eroded the gold from the foothills' quartz veins and beds of ancient rivers, and its riffles caught the flakes and nuggets to touch off the California Gold Rush, the greatest mass of migration of its kind in world history.

Those same waters, meeting the waters of the Sacramento in winter flood times and backing up to drop their loads of silt, built up the fertile lands on which the renewable wealth of agriculture was based.

After the Gold Rush, Sutter's Fort was forgotten, but the American River continued to play an important role in Sacramento's development.

But the rivers were no respecters of humankind. The Nisenan, over thousands of years, had learned to live with the American River. They harvested its salmon, gathered the berries and seeds and dug the roots of the plants along its banks, hunted the elk and deer and antelope that grazed in the river bottoms and over the vast floodplains.

In the hot valley summer, as the river dwindled to a warm trickle, the Nisenan left their villages for the cooler slopes of the Sierra. In wet winters, they sought nearby high ground to escape the floods that replenished the soil.

With the growth of Sacramento and as floods continued, drastic means seemed

Carmichael school teacher Effie Yeaw, for whom the nature center in Ancil Hoffman Park is named, introduced countless school children to nature while campaigning for creation of the American River Parkway.

called for. The river channel itself was moved and straightened. And the whole lower end of Sacramento was filled with cart loads of rubble to raise the streets and commercial buildings a story higher. By the 1920s, victory was declared, though the rivers still went on an occasional rampage every ten years or so. And having tamed the wild stallion, we decided to ride it. Dams were built and waterworks constructed.

Nowadays, we — the U.S. Bureau of Reclamation, abetted by a host of state and local water agencies — seek to manage the river from Folsom Dam, in flood times and drought, striving to balance often-competing municipal, agricultural and wildlife needs.

The wild river we have "conquered" is now more like an animal kept in a zoo. Water is released into it at our whim, for reasons having to do with economics, not the laws of nature. Salmon and steelhead spawning beds are left high and dry, or flooded out, with too little regard for the needs of the fish.

Mansions slip past the planning watchdogs and pop up all along the river, each taking a little nip out of the parkway that was established to protect and preserve the river and the tiny bit of riparian habitat that remains.

Sacramento, like most of the older cities of the world, owes its origin to a river. But again like most of the others, it has tended to turn its back on that river, as commerce and transportation turned from river to road and rail and switched from water power to steam and electricity.

Most cities have done worse than we, allowing their rivers to degenerate into virtual sewers and dumps. In Sacramento, we have at least tried to preserve ours, as a parkway for river-oriented recreation, for scenic values, and to protect a remnant of our wild heritage in the midst of a million-point-three population and climbing.

We have done these things reasonably well; we have a parkway that is continuous and virtually intact for 31½ miles, from beyond Folsom Dam to the mouth of the river at Discovery Park. And the parkway is popular; drawing tens of thousands of people annually to this 4,600-acre, mid-metropolis retreat. We have set an example that many other cities are now seeking to emulate.

But the environmental battle is never finally won; "eternal vigilance" is the never-ending watchword of those who believe the parkway is to Sacramento what Central Park is to New York. The purpose of this book is not simply to revisit dead events that may be of interest only academically.

For the American River and the Parkway are also memorials to Sacramento's history. The American is a place of history, from the Nisenan to Jed Smith and his fur trappers to Fremont and Kit Carson and James Marshall and John Sutter, to the early gold miners who swarmed over Sailor Bar and Mississippi Bar and those who later dredged up vast acres of cobbles, and the Chinese who ground-sluiced those mysterious tunnels near Folsom; to heroic efforts to cope with the river, and sometimes misguided efforts to manage it; to the Midwesterners lured out here to grow olives and oranges in "colonies" accented by the imported palm trees that today remain as the only evidence of their existence.

It is a history we need to remember, for it tells us who we are. With words and pictures, perhaps we can recall and remind, and possibly inspire Sacramento to rededicate itself to preserving this vital part of its own history.

In presenting this history, that is our hope.

Old gravel-hauling bridge, renamed Jim Jones Bridge to honor the SARA activist, accommodates bikers, fishermen and photographers.

Chapter 1

The First People

Lively, lively, we are lots of people
— Maidu Dance Song

The first occupants of the American River drainage lived in a much different environment from what we know today. Prehistorically, the Sacramento Valley was a tidal marsh covered by tule reeds, willows, and rushes. Other river vegetation included grapevines, roses, lupines, soaproot, tarweed, ragweed, brodiaea, and grasses.

This dense and varied vegetation provided habitat for many animal species, from the tule elk, antelopes, black bears, grizzly bears, deer, and wildcats to small rodents such as gophers, wood rats, and squirrels. The river banks sheltered beavers and river otters. Waterfowl included ducks, geese, cranes, herons, pelicans, and swans. In the uplands, there were quail, mourning doves, flickers, woodpeckers, roadrunners, hawks, owls, eagles, turkey vultures, and even condors. At least 26 species of fish lived in the American River. Most notable were the salmon, sturgeon, chub, tule perch, sucker, and trout.

Earliest Inhabitants

There is no definite archaeological evidence to support how the first inhabitants reached California. However, a combination of two hypotheses suggests a reasonable answer: Hypothesis 1. They came from Siberia when Pleistocene glaciation dropped ocean levels, creating a land bridge to Alaska. Nomadic hunters followed herds of large animals down an ice free corridor into the Great Basin area of North America, and then westward across the continent to California. Hypothesis 2 suggests that seafaring people from as far away as Japan moved northward along the Asian coast, fishing and gathering shellfish, and up over the land bridge to the North American coast, then down the coast to California and beyond to the tip of South America

While the initial movement into California was once thought to have occurred 1,500 years ago, it is now suggested that there has been continuous occupation for at least 4,500 years, with fragmentary evidence of as long as 12,000 years found in the Sierra.

The Central Valley's earliest settlers chose to live near a year-round supply of water at an elevation that would provide protection from seasonal floods. Usually their villages were also near oak groves that provided acorns for an important food supply. Today these first sites may no longer be found near a present water course. Floods and silting often brought the level of the river up to the base of the village sites and the occupants were forced to move their homes to escape flooding. Later the rivers shifted location and villages were built in new areas, again near the water.

The first people were mostly hunters of the large herds of deer, antelope and elk found in the river drainages. Their hunting implements (projectile points) were large and heavy, formed from slate, chert and obsidian Their diet also included plants and seeds that were ground up by placing them on a metate, a flat piece of stone, and grinding them with a smaller stone called a mano.

Beads made from abalone and olivella shells from the Pacific Ocean and traded from coastal communities are found at all early sites and beyond.

Eventually, the predominent method of acquiring food shifted from large mammals to a fishing economy. Large-scale harvesting of salmon and other migrating fish provided a dependable source of food and allowed for increased populations along river banks. Examination of skeletal remains indicated low infant mortality and greater adult longevity.

Projectile points were smaller and lighter, designed for use on an arrow shaft. By the 18th century, European items had been traded to the Indians of the river drainage by neighboring native populations.

The period from 1500 to 1769 when Spain established the first mission in San Diego marked the beginning of Western influence in California.

Archaeological Sites

Forty archaeological sites have been recorded on the banks of the American River from its mouth to the junction of the middle and south forks, now inundated by Folsom

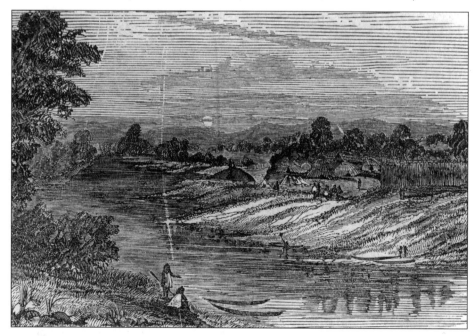

Nisenan settlements like this were scattered along most of the waterways in the area, including many on the American River.

Dam. These sites vary from large villages to bedrock mortar sites (grinding holes in the natural bedrock). The dominant village was Pujune, which extended from a few miles south of the mouth of the American to above the mouth of the Feather River. Others were Kadema and Yusumne near modern Watt Avenue.

In 2003, some 75,000 Indian artifacts and 45 parcels of human remains dating back more than 4,500 years were unearthed during a Sacramento City Hall expansion project. The artifacts were believed to have been from a sand dune village. Among them were fish weights, fish hooks and odd stones about two inches in diameter, and shaped like crescent moons. Archaeologists believe they may have been mounted on arrow shafts and used as a weapon to stun ducks.

Nisenan

Life Style

The Nisenan were the southernmost of three groups known as the Maidu. Nisenan is a word meaning "from among us; of our side." The term "Nisenan" was first used in the literature by Stephen Powers in 1877 when he described the group. Anthropologists based names of Indian groups on linguistic differences, but in fact the people lived in family groups that other cultures might designate as the "Jones Village" and "the Johnson Village" and the "Smith Village."

Boundaries

The Nisenan occupied the area from the eastern side of the Sacramento River to the 3,000-foot level of the Sierra Nevada. Their territory extended from the Bear and Yuba rivers to the vicinity of the Cosumnes, and included the entire American River drainage area. Although they may have used the higher areas in the Sierra for seasonal hunting, fishing, and gathering, no permanent settlements are known above 3,000 feet.

Settlements

Villages in the valley were located near running water or permanent springs. To provide protection from seasonal flooding, the villages were built on natural knolls or on mounds constructed for house sites. A southwestern exposure was important for warmth. Open country surrounding the village provided both habitat for large game animals and visibility in which to recognize approaching strangers.

A small village consisted of three to seven houses and a total population of 15 to 25 individuals. Larger villages may have had over 500 inhabitants. Several villages may have clustered around a large village with a headman who was empowered to call on neighboring villages on matters of mutual concern. Sometimes feuds erupted over trespassing or hunting rights, prompting a family to move to another village.

Two types of structures were built in the villages. The dwelling or *hu* was a dome-shaped structure built with a pole frame and covered with brush or tules and with earth. These dwellings were 10 to 15 feet in diameter. The ceremonial house (*kum*) was a larger semi-subterranean structure three-to-four feet in depth, built with heavy beams and covered by earth, tules, and brush. These *kums* were only in larger villages, or were shared by a group of small villages. A third type of structure, the sweathouse, was also found in some areas.

Subsistence

The Nisenan were hunters, gatherers, and fishermen, and blessed with year-around food sources. In the winter, late fall, and early spring, all members of a village were gathered together, but in the summer and early fall, part of the population moved to foothills or mountains in search of food.

During the winter the Nisenan hunted by stalking game or setting snares. In the summer they gathered seeds or hunted by setting nets over drying water holes to capture small birds and mammals. Deer were captured by burning dry grass in a circle around them and then shooting them when they were surrounded.

The land occupied by the valley and hill Nisenan provided their entire food supply. The Nisenan living on the Lower American River supplied roots for baskets, fresh water mollusks, salmon, antelope meat, other dried fish, and white-oak acorns. In return the hill Nisenan provided dried deer and bear meat, hides, rabbit-skin blankets, black-oak acorns, sugar-pine nuts, manzanita berries, tobacco, and the feathers of the red-shafted flicker and acorn woodpecker.

Gathering acorns was a family or village-wide affair. Men would knock the acorns from the trees and women and children would gather them for storage in a granary. Later they would be removed, cracked on an acorn anvil, shelled, and ground into flour on a bedrock mortar. A soaproot brush would be used to control scattering. Tannin would be removed by leaching. Using two sticks, fire-heated stones were dropped into water-tight baskets to cook the flour. Enough mush or soup was prepared to last several days. (Wilson, Towne).

Clothing and Decoration

During the summer months, the Nisenan needed little protective clothing. Common

Since the Nisenan had no pottery, they heated water for cooking by dropping hot stones into water-tight baskets.

A native American fandango.

apparel for women was an apron made from pounded willow or maple bark or from tules. Woven into two pieces, the apron was shorter in front, and was tucked between the legs when sitting. Men wore deer or rabbit skins with the hair side next to their flesh. On colder days, duck-feather or rabbit-skin blankets were worn.

Weapons

Bows were made from gray pine or cedar and were scraped and bound with deer sinew. The sinew was either pounded or soaked and chewed to make it soft enough to bind the bow. Arrows were made from hardwood or from a particular marsh plant, and usually had three feathers tied to the shaft. Points were fashioned from obsidian, stone or chert. Spears, used only in war, were made from willow and also had obsidian points.

Culture

A man usually obtained a woman's consent to marriage before approaching her parents for permission to wed. Then he would send beads and shells and food to show he would be a good provider. If the family accepted him, he would live with them and hunt and fish for them. After six months he and the woman went to live with his parents.

Either party could declare divorce. The most common cause was adultery A man was justified to kill his wife's lover or walked out. While he avoided his ex-spouse, he stayed on friendly terms with the family except his sister-in-law. Children went to the husband's family and were often adopted by the grandparents.

The Missions 1769-1839

The Mission period coincides with the era of Spanish control in California. In the beginning, it was a time of exploration and trapping by different European groups. During this time there were scattered contacts with the local Indians on the American River. In the years between 1805 and 1817, Gabriel Moraga, son of Jose Moraga (first commandant of the presidio of San Francisco), led a number of expeditions into the great valley. In 1806, he traveled north along the Sacramento River and "found multitudes of Indians everywhere along the streams." Two years later, he is believed to have reached the American River which, he noted, "carried more water than any others except the San Joaquin." Near the mouth of the American, he found the Indians hostile.

In honor of Christ's suffering on the cross Moraga named the American "Rio de las Llagas (river of sorrows)."

Strong opposition by the Miwok tribes on the Sacramento River blocked further advances of the missions, and missionization of the Nisenan never actually took place. Baptismal lists show only one Pujune Nisenan from the American River, an individual baptized in 1822.

However, local natives who had been brought into the missions often ran away, pursued by Spanish or Mexican soldiers. The people took refuge within the interior, including the area around the American River, bringing a knowledge of western culture and ideas and a fear of capture and enslavement. They also brought with them the Spanish language, which provided a unifying characteristic among people who spoke different languages. And Spanish raids on the interior for converts for the missions similarly influenced American River native populations.

Jedediah Strong Smith, the fur trader and explorer who was the first American trapper to reach the Central Valley, reached the American River in April, 1827 before making the first recorded crossing of the Sierra Nevada. During his two trips to the American he explored the same areas of the riparian forest that is today's American River Parkway and bicycle trail that bears his name.

Smith wrote of his meeting with the Indians on his return to the American the following year. He gave them gifts as a gesture of goodwill but they became frightened and fled. Others surrounded some of his men, and they fired, killing one and wounding another. Smith rode after others to offer gifts. When one of them fell, he found to his amazement that it was a girl of 14 or 15 and she was dead.

"Could it be possible," he wrote, "that we who called ourselves Christians were such frightful objects as to scare poor savages to death?" He left gifts and covered her with a blanket.

"...in commemoration of the singular wildness of these Indians and the novel occurrence that made it appear so forcibly, I named the River on which it happened Wild River."

Perhaps the most significant occurrence during the Mission period was the malaria epidemic of 1830-1833. It first appeared on the Columbia River in 1830 and reached the Central Valley in 1833. It is thought to have been introduced by ships docking at Fort Vancouver, and spread to California by trapping parties. Epidemics of malaria, along with measles, smallpox and other diseases to which the Indians had no resistance wiped out more than half of the California natives before they had even seen a white settler. The epidemics are estimated to have caused a 75 percent reduction in the native population of the Central Valley, leaving 20,000 persons dead in 1833.

John Augustus Sutter 1839-1850

Destruction of the California Indians by malaria opened the way for Western influence in the Sacramento Valley. Settlement started with the arrival in 1839 of John Augustus Sutter after a circuitous journey from Switzerland to carry out his dream of building a baronial estate in the new world. After becoming a Mexican citizen, he received a 48,400-acre land grant from Governor Alvarado who wanted to discourage Indian raiding and counter the growing power of his uncle, Mariano Guadalupe Vallejo, operating out of Sonoma as commander of the northern frontier.

With a party of 10 Hawaiians, several trappers and an Indian boy from the Rockies, Sutter sailed up the Sacramento River in three boats. They saw no Indians until reaching the upper delta, 12 miles south of the American River, where 200 painted Miwok men confronted them. Sutter waded ashore and sought to reassure them of his peaceful intentions, saying he only wanted to live among them and gave them presents. The Miwoks provided Sutter with a guide to lead them north into Nisenan country and out of their territory.

The party sailed on to the American River and upstream a short distance to land on the south shore at the foot of what is 28th street in Sacramento, a mile or so north of the knoll where he was to build his fort.

Sutter's ability to establish the first permanent non-native settlement in the Sacramento Valley when others had failed raises the question: how did he accomplish it? Certainly the impact of epidemics was an over-arching cause. But archivist Steve Beck of Sutter's Fort State Historic Park hypothesizes that factors of the valley Indian culture and Sutter's own character contributed to his success. Unlike the warlike Sioux and Apaches to the east, Sacramento Valley conflicts usually involved each side squaring off with bonfires, music, dancing and screaming, with the winner decided by who put on the best show.

Mode of traveling.

This type of fighting was called "posturing," and Beck writes that it fits with Sutter's own character. He claimed to be a captain in the elite Swiss Guard of Charles X, but while he may have served in the Swiss military, he was never an officer. He was educated in a military academy, he had a military bearing and he spoke four languages. He knew the importance of "putting up a good front."

When he arrived at the confluence of the Sacramento and American rivers in 1839 and was confronted by several hundred hostile natives, he had something earlier intruders did not have – three cannons purchased from the Hudson's Bay Company. As the natives charged on his small party, he fired his cannon, each loaded with three pounds of canister shot – at the opposite side of the river away from the natives. With a deafening roar and a cloud of smoke the shot obliterated several cottonwoods. The natives halted their charge and stood frozen. They had never seen such a powerful force; it was a form of "posturing" that played into Indian fighting style.

Sutter's thunderous arrival helped enlist the Indian population as his allies. Natives built the fort, made up his army and his labor force. They were his most trusted employees. Unlike the Spanish and Mexican mission and ranchero system had done, Sutter did not enslave the natives. He gave payment directly to the "Big Man (chief)" of each rancheria that supplied him with laborers. He gained trust with the natives by paying for the land on which his fort was built.

"Without the help of the natives Sutter would have never successfully settled in the Sacramento Valley," Steve Beck writes.

Although Sutter had relatively few problems with the weakened native population, there were times when he was forced to show his strength. The following is an account from his diary:

> "In the Spring 1840 the Indians began to be troublesome all around me, killing and wounding Cattle, stealing horses, and threatening to attack us en Masse. I was obligated to make Campaigns against them and punish them severely; a little later about 2a 300 was approaching and got United on Consume River, but I was not waiting for them … The fighting was a little hard, but after having lost about 30 men, they was willing to make a treaty with me, and after this lecon, they behaved very well, and became my best friends and Soldiers, with which I has been assisted to conquer the whole Sacramento and a part of the San Joaquin Valley."

Catching Grasshoppers.

With the exception of this incident, a similar one in 1841, and a Mokelumne raid in 1846, Sutter had a peaceful working relationship with the Nisenan and Miwok tribelets. At first the Indians remained close to New Helvetia, where they received a variety of goods in return for their labor. But between 1843 and 1846 there was considerable movement of Nisenan villages. In 1847 disease again reduced the valley population.

Early in the Sutter period, Nisenan villages were scattered along the American and Sacramento rivers near New Helvetia. Charles Wilkes, U.S. naval expedition leader, describes their lodges as being similar to "haycocks made of sticks and bulrush." In 1846 over 300 Indians were harvesting wheat for Sutter. But within three years diseases and the onslaught of gold miners and settlers decimated the valley Nisenan population on the American River.

American Period 1850-1900

The American Period begins with the Gold Rush and ends with the virtual disappearance of native culture in the Central Valley by the end of the 19th century.

The gold discovery site at Coloma was near the geographic center of Nisenan territory, and the Nisenan were among the first to feel an impact. Already weakened by the epidemics of 1833 and 1847, the Nisenan could offer little resistance when in 1848 Sutter began using them as a labor force for his mining operations. This practice was followed by other settlers.

In 1850 the Nisenan and Miwok waged sporadic raids against isolated settlers in a futile campaign. For the next 10 years their villages were burned and the people hunted like animals. With their native lands overrun, some found work on ranches and in mining. In 1859 the entire Indian population of Sacramento, El Dorado, and Placer counties was estimated at only 3,500.

From 1870-1890 a few individuals gathered in camps and attempted to restore their culture through a series of revivals, including the Ghost Dance and annual ceremonies. These efforts were unsuccessful; with intermarriage among the Indian groups becoming common, knowledge of the old ways faded or was modified.

Today, more and more people are proud of whatever Indian heritage they may have; the number of people who say they have Indian blood in California is approaching the number of Indians who lived here at the time the Spanish started the first mission. In 2005, State Parks officials were working with tribal groups on plans for a major state museum of Indian culture and history in the American River Parkway.

Grinding Acorns.

Rancho life was built around the huge herds of cattle that grazed the open range. Californios were renowned for their riding skills — and sometimes their careless cruelty — as in this sport of the Carrera de Gallo in which a half-buried rooster is snatched up by a galloping horseman.

Chapter 2

Hispanic Period

… If the men who hoisted the "Bear Flag" had raised the flag that Washington sanctified by his abnegation and patriotism, there would have been no war on the Sonoma frontier, for all our minds were prepared to give a brotherly embrace to the sons of the Great Republic, whose enterprising spirit had filled us with admiration. …
— *Mariano Guadalupe Vallejo*

California's Hispanic Period encompasses the years between 1542 with the discovery of Alta California by seafarer Juan Rodriguez Cabrillo under the sponsorship of Spanish conquistador Hernando Cortes, to the conquest of California by the United States in 1846. During this time, both Spain and Mexico conducted exploration and settlement expeditions, establishing Hispanic hegemony over the land and its people.

Spanish Explorations

Spanish settlement in Alta California was confined to a thin coastal strip. Except for two short-lived establishments on the Colorado River in the vicinity of modern-day Yuma, Arizona, the greatest distance to which the Spanish penetrated inland was 30 miles.

Prior to the Gold Rush, the great Central Valley was described by historian Hubert Howe Bancroft as being "more land than men." There were never more than 7,000 people in California. As late as 1847, John Sutter noted in his Helvetia Diary that only 289 white settlers were living in the Sacramento Valley.

Probably the first European to visit the Central Valley was Pedro Fages. This discovery came during an exploration trip from Monterey in 1772. Fages describes the expedition's route along the eastern edge of San Francisco Bay as passing "a round bay like great Lake (San Pablo) large enough for all the armadas of Spain." These first explorers were fascinated by the spouting whales in the bay. Fages was even given a kindly welcome, probably at Pinole Valley, by "bearded and light-complexioned" Indians.

The expedition intended to reach the north shore of the "round bay" (bahia redondo), but was stopped by Carquinez Strait. Here Fages climbed a hill and got a view of an unknown delta land of channels and islands leading toward what would one day be Sacramento. That's as close as he got to the American River.

After this abortive attempt there were periodic efforts to find suitable sites for missions in the interior. Although none was found, the Spanish did penetrate the interior to search for Indians who had run away from the missions and to recover livestock stolen by the Indians.

American Trappers

After Jedediah Smith's second visit to the Central Valley (Ch. 1), he went north, eventually reaching Fort Vancouver, headquarters for the Hudson's Bay Company. Smith's reports of the quality and quantity of furs along the banks of the American aroused the interest of the company, prompting it to send three expeditions into the region. They were led by Alexander McLeod in 1828-29, Peter Skene Ogden in 1829-30, and John Work in 1832-33.

John Work attempted to travel down the flooded Sacramento valley in winter by keeping to the foothills of the Sierras, but was forced to winter at the Sutter Buttes. On

Jedediah Smith was the first American in the Central Valley. He and his wandering band of beaver trappers are believed to have reached the American River in April 1827.

January 10, 1833, Work made the following note in a journal while in the camp near the south fork of the American:

> The people who slept out arrived with 10 beaver. The man who remained behind had a trap and a beaver stolen by the Indians. The Indians are very quiet when they see people altogether, but when they find only one or two people by themselves, their conduct alters. Several people went out hunting, without success, there are tracks of a chance deer and some antelope but not a vestige of elk nor did we mark of any during these two days journey.
>
> The deer and elk are so shy that they cannot be approached. When Mr. (Peter Skene) Ogden passed here there were plenty of elk, it is singular there are none now. Not finding elk here as we expected is a great disappointment as many of the people have very little to eat.
>
> The big river cannot be crossed below as the plain on the other side is all under water. The Americans had crossed and were obliged to come back again & also are coming this way.
>
> Under the circumstances we must also turn back where we may find some elk to subsist on."

In May 1833 Captain John R. Cooper petitioned Jose Figueroa, Mexican governor of California, for a tract of land along the American. In his petition, and accompanying "diseno" (map), Cooper identified the American as the "Rio Ojotska" which is the phonetic spelling of the Russian word for "hunter". Cooper received the grant but reduced his claim in 1835 in favor of another grant, the Rancho el Molino in Sonoma county.

In 1837 the American River was given its permanent name by Governor Alvarado, who called it the "Rio do los Americanos" because the area was frequented by "trappers of revolutionary proclivities."

The familiar story of John Augustus Sutter (Chapter 1) and his plan of empire began in August 1839. Sutter traveled up the Sacramento River from Yerba Buena (San Francisco) on the schooner *Isabella* and landed on the south bank of the American near present 28th and B streets on August 15, 1839.

Although Alvarado was actually first to name the river, Sutter has often been given the credit. This was based on an interview Sutter gave to the historian Bancroft in 1876:

> I gave the name American River to the stream that bears it now from the fact that about three miles above the Fort was a pass (ford) where the Canadian trappers, who were called Americanos by the Spanish-speaking Indians, crossed the stream.
>
> This place was called El Paso de los Americanos so I called this stream the American River.

Much of our knowledge of the valley during this period comes from the diaries and journals of explorers and travelers. In 1841 Charles Wilkes led the United States Exploring Expedition through California. In his narrative Wilkes makes these comments on the American River:

> The American River is a small branch that joins the Sacramento at New Helvetia. New Helvetia is bounded on the North by the American Fork, a small serpentine stream which has a course but of a few miles. This river having a bar near its mouth, no vessels larger than boats can enter it.

Other settlers soon began to join Sutter along the American. John Yates, master of Sutter's schooner *Sacramento*, recorded his visit to the valley and reported on some of the residents. He visited the Rancho del Paso of Eliab Grimes on the north bank of the American opposite Sutter's Fort:

> Pursuing my journey along the valley the next settlement I came to was Captain Grimes' Rancho on the American River. The house was constructed of mud and roofed with tule after the manner of all the first dwellings of the settlers in this section of the country.
>
> Grimes had, I learned, gone to the Sandwich Islands and a Mr. Sinclair was

John Augustus Sutter had to pledge loyalty to the Mexican government to obtain his land grant on the American River. Even though he served as the local military governor under the Mexican regime, he welcomed all comers to his fort.

left in charge of affairs of the Rancho. I found the latter a talented man and a capital company where grog and cards were stirring. He was particularly fond of both these exciting games.

Mexican Land Grants

Rancho del Paso had been granted to Grimes in 1844 by Governor Manuel Micheltorena. This tract included 44,000 acres extending for eight miles along the bank of the American and for eight and one-half miles north.

In 1843 a young Swedish scholar, Sandels, visited Sutter's Fort and surrounding the area. He, too, visited John Sinclair on the river:

> Mr. Sinclair, a partner with Captain Sutter in farming pursuits, and a Mr. Grimes, have a large productive farm on the American Fork. Mr. Sinclair is from Scotland, and is a very interesting gentleman in conversation and possesses a great enterprise in business. He was a hunter for many years among the Rocky Mountains, acting as a clerk for one of the Hudson's Bay Company's expedition.
>
> He treated me to a rural breakfast, and, in accordance with his old habits, broiled his meat on a ramrod stuck before the fire.
>
> The limpid and beautiful river near which his home is situated is made doubly attractive when compared with the sultry plains in the vicinity, upon which good water is not always to be obtained.

Another visitor to John Sinclair's was Edwin Bryant, who traveled from Kentucky to California in 1846. He recorded his September 1, 1846 visit:

> We reached the residence of John Sinclair, Esq., on the Rio de los Americanos, about two miles east of Sutter's Fort. The composition of the soil appears to be such as to render in highly productive, with proper cultivation, of the small grains.
>
> The ground is trodden up by immense herds of cattle and horses which grazed here in the early spring, when it was wet and apparently miry. We passed through large evergreen oak groves, some of them miles in width.
>
> Game is very abundant. We frequently saw deer feeding quietly one or two hundred yards from us, and large flocks of antelope.

Adjoining Grimes' El Paso grant to the east was the 22,000-acre San Juan Rancho of Joel P. Dedmond. On the opposite, or south bank, of the American, and adjoining Sutter's New Helvetia property was the 35,000 acre Rancho Rio de los Americanos of William A. Leidesdorff. Both the San Juan and Rio de los Americanos grants were approved by Governor Micheltorena in 1844.

One of the best descriptions of the American River descent into the Sacramento Valley during the 1840s was written by John C. Fremont. The following is from his 1844 journal:

> March 1. We made a pleasant camp on the river hill, where were some beautiful specimens of the chocolate-colored shrub (probably manzanita) which were a foot in diameter near the ground, and fifteen to twenty feet high. The opposite ridge runs continuously along, unbroken by stream. We are rapidly descending into the spring and we are leaving our snowy region far behind; everything is getting green; butterflies are swarming; numerous bugs are creeping out, wakened from their winter's sleep, and the forest flowers are coming into bloom. Among those which appeared most numerously today was *Dodecatheon Dentatum*. [More likely *hendersonii* — Ed.]
>
> March 3. At every step the country improved in beauty; the pines were rapidly disappearing and the oaks became the principal trees of the forest. Among

these, the prevailing tree was the evergreen oak, (which by way of distinction, we shall call the live oak) and with these occurred frequently a new species of oaks bearing a long slender acorn, from an inch to an inch and a half in length, which we now began to see formed the principal vegetable food of the inhabitants of this region. In a short distance we crossed a little rivulet, where two old huts stood, and nearby were heaps of acorn hulls. The ground round about was very rich, covered with an exhuberant sward of grass … We followed on a trail; still keeping out of the river and descended to a very large creek, dashing with great velocity over a pre-eminently rocky bed and among large boulders. The bed had sudden breaks, formed by deep holes and ledges of rock running across. Even here, it deserves the name of Rock Creek, which we gave it. We succeeded in fording, and toiled about three thousand feet up the opposite hill. The mountains were getting sensibly lower, but still there is valley on the river, which presents steep and rocky banks; but here several miles from the river, the valleys of rivulets, or around spring heads, the low groves of live Oak give the appearance of orchards in an old cultivated country. Occasionally we met deer, but had not the necessary time for hunting.

March 4. Our road led along a ridge inclining to the river, and the air in the open grounds was fragrant with flowering shrubs; and in the morning we issued on an open spur, by which we descended down to the stream. Here the river issues suddenly from the mountains, which hitherto had hemmed it closely in; these now became softer and changed sensibly their character and at this point commences the most beautiful valley in which we have ever traveled … We encamped in the evening on the shore of the river, at a place where the associated beauties of scenery made so strong an impression on us that we have given it the name Beautiful Camp [said to have been Coloma — Ed] … The undulating river shore was shaded with live oaks, which forms a continuous grove, and the same grassy sward extended to the edge of the river; and we made fires near some large granite masses which were among the trees.

Fremont's cartographer, Charles Preuss, also kept a diary of the trip along the American. He became separated from the main party for a few days, during which time he made the following notes:

February 29. Under the circumstances I feel quite satisfied in this magnificent spring weather and mountain air. The water gurgles at my feet; green trees, live oaks and many kinds of conifers all around.

March 1. We moved on a few miles and turned again toward the main stream, where a little more grass is to be found. The path is slippery because of the dry fir needles. What weather. Everything has started to sprout. Butterflies fly about, also mosquitos, beetles and ants. Everything is alive. The white snow-covered mountains are already quite a distance behind us.

March 2. The eternal going up and down hill is so exhausting that I'd rather camp here by the water at a good fire and suffer a little hunger than to continue to run around in these rocks and mountains.

March 3. This is beginning to get serious. I couldn't find the others and I am here alone. Since yesterday morning I have not eaten a thing except a few sweet onions which I just scratched out of the ground. At the same time, I found an ant's nest, a portion of which I bit off and swallowed. Nor do I have any tobacco. How will this end?

Fortunately, all was to end well, with no loss of life. Fremont and his exploring party spent two weeks at Sutter's Fort and on the 22nd of March, moved camp across the American on the Rancho del Paso in preparation for the return east.

Chapter 3

Conquest Of California

We are a marvel to ourselves and a miracle to the world. . .
— *Peter Burnett, first governor of California*

Those who came to Hispanic California, whether to trade, trap, or explore, almost universally admired what they saw. Like Fremont, they viewed California as being "surpassingly beautiful." For some, California was the place where good land and plenty of it could be had for the asking. For others it represented the fulfillment of our Manifest Destiny; a Union of States stretching from the Atlantic to the Pacific. Whatever the view, as more accounts of California began to circulate in the East, more Americans decided to make the trek West.

Emigrants

In the years following Fremont's 1844 expedition, American emigrants began coming to California in ever-increasing numbers. Most of those who came overland followed the central route. For these, Sutter's Fort was their first encounter with civilization in California. The sight of the adobe-walled fort signaled the end of months of hardship, danger and privation.

The American flag was raised over Sutter's Fort in July of 1846.

To the many immigrants who needed his aid, Sutter was always the great provider. He wrote later:

> Now came the surging flood of immigration, accompanied often by hunger, death and distress. At times my buildings were filled with emigrants. So much so that I could scarcely find a spot to lay my own head to rest.
>
> My farm-house and store-houses were filled every winter during these immigration times with poor, wet, hungry men, women and children seeking a fortune in a new land.
>
> They were of my breed and they loved the promise of the soil. Often it was necessary for me to go with my men and cattle to drag them into safety out of the snow.
>
> These poor usually arrived in a destitute condition and hard indeed would have been the man who demanded payment for shelter, food, or clothing. Very few possessed more than their teams when they arrived. They came to my Fort with nothing but their tired bodies and their rainwet clothing.

Of the four relief expeditions sent out to rescue the survivors of the Donner-Reed party, two were from Sutter's Fort. The first of these set out on February 4, some 14 strong; only seven had the strength to complete the trip. After two weeks the first party returned to the fort. The last of the relief attempts in April was mainly one of salvage. Of the 82 original members of the Donner-Reed party, only 47 reached Sutter's Fort alive.

Bear Flag Revolt

While the epic story at Donner Lake was unfolding, events were transpiring in the valley below that were to bring fundamental change to California. In the spring of 1846, American settlers in the Great Valley came to believe that Mexican officialdom was hostile to their presence. To forestall their expected expulsion from California, the settlers organized the Bear Flag revolt and marched on Sonoma, June 14, 1846.

Settlers "captured" General Mariano Vallejo at his residence in Sonoma and declared the Independent Republic of California. Vallejo and his brother Salvador, Victor Purdon and Vallejo's Yankee brother-in-law Jacob Leese were taken to Sutter's Fort and held prisoner there until August. After his release, Vallejo, characterized by some as the Americans' best friend in California, returned to Sonoma and burned his Mexican uniforms. He foresaw the end of Mexican rule in California.

Other events were to quickly overshadow the actions of the "Bear-Flaggers." On July 7, 1846, shortly after the official declaration of war between Mexico and the United States, Commodore Sloat raised the American flag at Monterey. Four days later, July 11, the flag was raised over Sutter's Fort.

About this period, John Bidwell wrote:

> The first conquest of California in 1846, by the Americans, with the exception of the skirmish at Petaluma and another towards Monterey, was achieved without a battle. We simply marched all over California from Sonoma to San Diego and raised the American flag without opposition or protest. We tried to find an enemy but could not.

Very little of significance occurred at Sutter's Fort during hostilities between the two countries. When "war" commenced Fremont was camped along the American River somewhere eight or ten miles from the river's mouth, perhaps in the vicinity of the present Howe Avenue Bridge. Fremont took command of Sutter's Fort and, while he himself went marching "all over California" the fort was placed under the charge of Edward Kern, topographical engineer.

One of Sutter's great passions was the pomp and ceremony of the military parade ground. For all of his life Sutter would seek the status of military rank. To be placed in a subordinated position in his own fort was a galling experience:

> I believed at first that these men (Fremont's Battalion) were to assist me, but I discovered soon that they were left to act as spies over me.

By January of 1847 American rule had come to California.

The year 1847 was a good one for Sutter. Activities connected with his fort were well established and prospering. Entries in the New Helvetian Diary illustrate his optimism for the future. Lumber was being cut in the foothills and rafted down the American. An entry for October 27 tells of 81 hides delivered that day to the tannery on the banks of the American. Sutter began the work of constructing a grist or flour mill upriver from the fort by contracting with some members of the disbanded Mormon Battalion who were on their way to Utah. The new mill would have a capacity of 40 bushels per hour, which would handle "what Sacramento Valley will be able to produce in wheat."

Only one thing was lacking. Sutter had the logs, now he needed some means of producing lumber which was more efficient than the primitive saw pit at the fort. Sutter and James Marshall agreed to a partnership in a sawmill, and in August, Marshall found the perfect spot for the mill. It was on the South Fork of the American River at a place known as Coloma.

Fremont recruited men at Sutter's Fort and marched them with his Battalion to Monterey to join with U.S. forces in the war with Mexico

Pack animals carried miners and their meager belongings on the last leg of their journey to "see the elephant."

Chapter 4

The Gold Rush

No time in the history of our country has presented such temptations to desert as now exist in California.
— Col. Richard Mason, U.S. military governor of California, Aug. 17, 1848

The Gold Rush instantly changed immigration to California from a trickle to a flood. San Francisco sprang from a quiet village to a world class seaport in a matter of months. Sacramento, the jumping-off point for the mines, expanded as tumultuously. Sutter and his dreams of empire were overwhelmed; even his carefully laid-out Sutterville on the Sacramento River (near today's William Land Park) was ignored for a makeshift landing at the foot of J Street. A city of tents and shacks burned and was rebuilt; burned again and rose once more; suffered floods in between, and through it all, grew inexorably. The growth of a settlement into a city, which might have taken two centuries in New England or Pennsylvania, took less than two years in Gold Rush California.

The Gold Discovery

Because he was the man who saw "something shining in the bottom of the ditch," James Marshall's place in history is secure:

> While we were in the habit at night of turning the water through the tail race we had dug for the purpose of widening and deepening the race, I used to go down in the morning to see what had been done by the water through the night; and about half past seven o'clock on or about the 19th day of January — I am not quite certain to a day, but it was between the 18th and 20th of that month — 1848, I went down as usual, and after shutting off the water from the race I stepped into it, near the lower end, and there upon the rock, about six inches beneath the surface of the water, I discovered the gold.
>
> I was entirely alone at the time. I picked up one or two pieces and examined them attentively; having some general knowledge of minerals, I could not call to mind more than two which in any way resembled this — sulphuret of iron, very bright and brittle; and gold, bright, yet malleable.
>
> I then tried it between two rocks and found that it could be beaten into a different shape, but not broken.
>
> I then collected four or five pieces and went to Mr. Scott (who was working at the carpenter's bench making a mill wheel) with the five pieces and said, " I have found it."
>
> "What is it? inquired Scott.
>
> "Gold," I answered.

> I went to the Fort ... and carried with me about three ounces of the gold,
> which Capt. Sutter and I tested with nitric acid.

Marshall wrote this account almost 10 years after his momentous discovery. However, Henry Bigler, a Mormon workman at the mill, had noted the date of the discovery in his diary as January 24, 1848,

John Sutter saw the discovery as a threat to his empire at Sacramento. Hoping to keep the find a secret, Sutter rode eastward along the American to Coloma where he spoke with his laborers:

> I told them that I would consider it as a great favor if they would keep this discovery secret for only six weeks, so that I could finish my large flour mill at Brighton (with four run of stones), which had cost me already from 24 to 25,000 dollars — the people up there promised to keep it a secret so long.
> On my way home, instead of feeling happy and contented, I was unhappy, and could not see that it could benefit me much ...

Despite his misgivings about the benefit of Marshall's discovery, Sutter himself helped spread the news. He concluded a lease with the Indians at Coloma for his mill site, and sent a messenger to Monterey asking the military governor, Colonel R. B. Mason, to approve the lease. With the messenger, Sutter forwarded six ounces of gold.

Even though "Sutter's Secret" leaked out, there was no immediate stampede into the Sierra. Rumors of gold had circulated in California since the days of the earliest explorations. There had even been a minor discovery in the southern part of the state in 1842.

It took a canny Mormon, Sam Brannan, to stir up the hornet's nest. Brannan had a store at the fort and very soon was aware of the discovery. This future millionaire was never one to neglect an opportunity, and recognized that Marshall's find could be turned to his own profit. Quietly Brannan began scouring the countryside, buying up supplies and equipment that would be needed by anyone who might dig for gold. When his purchases were safely in place at the fort, Brannan went to San Francisco. On May 12, with hat in one hand and a quinine bottle of gold dust in the other, Brannan ran through the street, war-whooping:

"Gold! Gold! Gold from the American River!"

The result was electric. Witness one observer's reaction:

> I looked on for a moment; a frenzy seized my soul; unbidden my legs performed some entirely new movements of polka steps — I took several — houses were too small for me to stay in; I was soon in the street in search of necessary outfits; piles of gold rose up before me at every step; castles of marble, dazzling the eye with their rich appliances; thousands of slaves bowing to my beck and call; myriads of fair virgins contending with each other for my love — were among the fancies of my fevered imagination. The Rothschilds, Girards, and Astors appeared to me but poor people; in short, I had a very violent attack of gold fever.

Although the excitement in California was very great, reports that reached the East were generally discounted as western exaggeration. Governor Mason came up to Sacramento in August, 1848 to visit the mining area along the American in order that he might forward a first-hand account to Washington. His subsequent report to the Secretary of War and a tea caddy or chest stuffed with 230 ounces of pure California gold on display at the War Department in Washington was enough to convince even the most skeptical easterner — and the rush was on.

Mason's report gives an excellent view of mining along the American and the state of affairs among the people in 1848:

> ... on the 5th (of August) resumed the journey from Sutter's and proceeded twenty-five miles up the American fork to a point on it and known as the Lower Mines, or Mormon Diggins. The hillsides were thickly strewn with canvas tents and bush arbors; a store was erected and several boarding shanties in operation.
>
> The day was intensely hot, yet about two hundred men were at work in the full glare of the sun washing for gold — some with tin pans, some with closely woven Indian baskets, but the greater part had a rude machine, known as the cradle ...
>
> Mr. Sinclair, whose ranch is 3 miles above Sutter's on the north side of the American, employs about 50 (Indians) on the North Fork not far from the junction with the main stream. He had been engaged about five weeks when I saw him, and up to that time his Indians have simply used closely woven willow baskets. His net proceeds were about $16,000 worth of gold. He showed me the proceeds of his last week's work — 14 pounds of avoirdupois of clean washed gold.
>
> The discovery of these deposits of gold has entirely changed the character of Upper California. Its people, before engaged in cultivating their small patches of ground and guarding their herds of cattle and horses, have all gone to the mines, or are on their way thither; laborers of every trade have left their work, and tradesmen their shops; sailors desert their ships as fast as they arrive on the coast, and several vessels have gone to sea with hardly enough hands to spread a sail; two or three are now at anchor in San Francisco with no crews on board.
>
> Many desertions too, have taken place from the garrisons within the influence of the mines. I shall spare no exertions to apprehend and punish deserters, but I believe no time in the history of our country has presented such temptations to desert as now exist in California.
>
> It may be a matter of surprise why I have made no report on this subject at an earlier date. The reason is, that I could not bring myself to believe the reports that I heard of the wealth of the gold district until I visited it myself. I have no hesitation now in saying that there is more gold in the country ... than will pay the cost of the present war with Mexico a hundred times over.

In later years John Sutter was to recall that his worst fears about the future of his beloved New Helvetia were realized:

> As soon as the secret was out my laborers began to leave me, in small parties first, but then all left, from the clerk to the cook, and I was in great distress; only a few mechanics remained to finish some very necessary work, which they had commenced, and about eight invalids, who continued slowly to work a few teams, to scrape out the mill race at Brighton.
>
> What a great misfortune was this sudden gold discovery for me. It has just broken up and ruined my hard, restless and industrious labors, connected with many dangers of life, as I had many narrow escapes before I became properly established.
>
> From my mill buildings I reaped no benefit whatever, the mill stones even have been stolen and sold.

It was not understood at first how widespread the gold fields were. Coloma and the "American Fork" were the central magnets which drew the first miners. As other discoveries were made, a theory gained currency that there was a "Mother Lode." It was supposed that during a long-ago period of volcanic eruption in the Sierra, a gigantic mountain of gold heated up, and pieces of molten gold were showered over the countryside. Most of the mountain was still intact, waiting ...

Many a prospecting party set out to search for this El Dorado of El Dorados; and to their restless wanderings may be greatly attributed the extraordinarily rapid extension of the gold field. (Bancroft)

The results of these "restless wanderings" can still be seen; a few of the early camps have become cities, others remain as quaint villages, most are simply grass-grown heaps of tailings.

Geology

American River gold is mostly placer gold. The story of how it came to be is one that spans hundreds of millions of years and is bound inextricably with the sometimes slow, sometimes violent formation of the land.

Three hundred million years ago Sacramento County was part of an extensive inland sea. Then about 130 million years ago, the flat sea floor was twisted into a series of folds and fused by heat into a solid mass of rock.

At this time the beginnings of the Sierra Nevada thrust upward, shattering the solid mass and creating fissures in it. Superheated liquids carrying gold and other minerals welled upward from the earth's molten interior, filling the fissures and here and there forming veins of gold. Over more millions of years erosion worked its slow process of wearing away the rock. As the gold veins were exposed, minute particles of the gold were carried away, occasionally in nugget-sized chunks. Flakes and chunks alike were carried down the mountain slopes to be deposited little by little in sand bars, gravel beds and river bottoms — forming the rich placers which were destined to focus a startled world's attention on California in 1848.

Mining Techniques

Many techniques were used to mine placer gold, but all are based on the law of gravity. Heavy gold is separated from lighter material by the uses of water.

Early miners were ignorant of geology and mineralogy and their equipment was primitive and inefficient. At first miners used a pan made of tin or sheet iron, which had a flat bottom and sides that sloped outward. The pan was dipped in the water and shaken

Miners working as a team with a long tom could process much more gravel than they could by prospecting alone with a pan.

from side to side, or rotated, floating away the dirt while the gold settled in the bottom of the pan. Stones were raked out by hand.

Very soon the panning process was replaced by the "rocker" or "cradle." This was a simple wooden trough with low sides and one open end. A square box, or hopper, was fitted atop the upper end. The perforated bottom of the hopper acted as a sieve. Under the hopper was an apron of wood or canvas which sloped from the bottom of the hopper to the upper end of the cradle.

Gold-bearing dirt was shoveled into the hopper and while the miner "rocked the cradle" with one hand, he poured water over the dirt with the other. Fine gold was retained on the apron, while heavier particles lodged behind wooden strips, or "riffle bars" nailed across the bottom of the cradle. Mud and water ran out the open end; most of the gold was retained either on the apron or on the bottom of the cradle box.

To handle greater volumes of gravel, the cradle was soon expanded into the "long tom," a double-decked sluice box with the top deck screened and the longer, lower deck fitted with cleats like the riffle bars of the cradle. It was a two-man affair; one shoveled the gravel onto the top deck, and the other man poured on the water and kept the gravel moving.

When there was enough flowing water from a stream or a system of ditches, miners came to prefer a plain sluice box, merely a long wooden trough with cleats in the bottom. The gravel was shoveled in the top, and the natural flow washed it through the sluice with the cleats catching the heavy gold particles. The longer the sluice, the better chance to catch the gold, so some sluices were hundreds of feet long, and elaborate ditch systems were constructed to provide the needed head of water.

These methods quickly replaced Gold Rush fiction's romantic figure of the lonely miner hunkered beside a mountain stream with his pan. For as systems became more complex, miners began to work in concert rather than as individuals. Early newspapers carry frequent announcements of companies forming or dissolving in the business of taking out gold.

Mining Camps

No matter what the system, mining for gold was a hard life, with few of the amenities of civilization. The men who lived in the long-gone miner's cabin that archaeologists have located at Sailor Bar, near the Hazel Avenue Bridge, would probably recognize the following 1873 description of a miner's life:

> ... black coffee, boiled beans, fried bacon, bread baked in a Dutch oven, or pancakes form their frugal meal. But it is eaten with a relish that an epicure would envy ... beside the cabin are utensils with which they pursue their daily toil.
>
> Now let us take a peep inside the cabin and see what the domestic arrangements are. Somewhat neater than one would suppose from the appearances of the outside. No paper or cloth on the walls to be sure, but the nails driven into the logs would spoil that.
>
> Four bunks on each side of the cabin, with their heads toward the door in a double tier. A small, rough table in the center with several boxes and powder kegs for chairs, a small looking-glass near the little window with a comb suspended from a string beside it.
>
> These catch the eye of the visitor at the first glance.
>
> Then he becomes cognizant of some sides of bacon suspended from a beam

— a miner's pan or two, an old pick handle, some store clothes hanging from nails, a couple of common trunks, and several cracker boxes and carpet sacks, in company with gum boots protrude from the lower bunks.

The walls are well ornamented with cuts taken from illustrated newspapers and a few photographs are tacked under two or three of the bunks.

On a couple of shelves over the fireplace are a few well-worn books, which show signs of hard service. An old newspaper sticks out of the foot of one of the bunks.

At the back of the cabin is the open fire place in front of which the boys sit on winter evenings. In the summer they prefer to sit outside around the camp fire and smoke their pipes, spin yarns, and dream of the time when they will have made their pile.

On another shelf above the window is a bag of salt, several yeast powder cans, a paper of coffee, a couple of bottles of quick-silver, some plugs of tobacco, and a worn pack of cards and crib boards.

In the corner is a bread pan, some molasses bottles, a demijohn and a pair of boots undergoing repairs.

The beds consist of a couple of pairs of blankets without sheets or coverlet, made up on a straw mattress, with a coat or two for a pillow. (*Pacific Rural Press* 1873)

As the search for gold spread from Coloma, other discoveries were made. Wherever there was a "strike" a mining community sprang up, only to fade away when the gold was gone. Sailor Bar was only one of these mining camps on the American within Sacramento County.

Mormon Island

On the South Fork of the American, very near the point where the North and South Forks join, was the mining town of Mormon Island. The camp took its name from the fact that its two discoverers were Mormons.

Mormon Island, the next place gold was found after the Discovery at Coloma, is now under the waters of Folsom Lake.

In the spring of 1848 while on their way to Sutter's mill at Coloma, Sidney Willis and Wilford Hudson, late of the Mormon battalion, camped on the bar "opposite a little island about half-way down the river." Their decision to do a little prospecting resulted in the discovery of the second important gold strike in California.

Sam Brannan, acting in his capacity as leader of the Mormons in California, filed a preemptive claim and mining got underway. Those who were working the claim gave notice they would brook no interference in their venture:

> Notice is hereby given that the residents of the junction at the North Fork and South Fork of the American River, having formed themselves into Company for the purpose of damning (sic) and turning the river from its original bed, this is to caution all persons from trespassing on their claim, as they are determined to defend it with their lives.

Less than a year later the determination of the Mormon Island Association to "defend (their claim) with their lives" was tested:

> Whereas, Charles Leonard, James Sargeant and Nathan English, three of the original members were unfortunately killed by Indians this spring, therefore resolved: half of each share shall be let out to anybody, and half is to be used by the heirs.

Sam Brannan opened a store in the mushrooming community and began a free ferry service across the river. In September of 1849 James Birch, pioneer California stage operator, began a stagecoach service between Sacramento and Mormon Island. A few months later, in February 1850, his business was so good that the line was extended to Coloma. Fare was two "ounces" ($32) one way.

Mormon Island proved an excellent claim. In less than a month four Mormons headed for Los Angeles with 100 pounds of gold. The Alta California reported:

> Near Mormon Island last week, three men took out $8,848 in three days. These mines are undoubtedly the most productive being worked.
> ... in 1850 a green hand took out nineteen thousand dollars in a period of three days, and three pounds of dust in just one afternoon.

By 1850 there were 1,500 miners working claims in the area, and plenty of enterprising merchants to make sure the miner had a place to spend his dust. There were even dazzling social events such as the famous Christmas Ball. Billed as the first ball in Sacramento county, this gala event was held December 25, 1849. Tickets went for $20 — half-price if one contributed to the refreshments. Ladies at the affair were:

> ... hale and buxom maidens with short dresses, grey woolen stockings, and brogans with soles a half inch thick.

The belle of the ball was a hefty 189-pound fourteen-year old beauty affectionately dubbed "the infant."

In 1853 Mormon Island's population reached 2,500 and the community entered its period of peak activity. Then in 1856, fire, the scourge of many a mining town, struck Mormon Island:

> Mrs. S. G. Elliott reports a fire on June 23, noon, at Mormon Island. It is believed to be the work of an incendiary, one of a number of local dangerous and superstitious characters.

A list of losses was printed the next day: Natoma Hotel, Tunis Bodine Bowling Alleys, Natoma Store, Sons of Temperance Hall, Temple of Honor, Darius King Bookstore.

The Wells Fargo office and the post office were the only buildings on Main Street not destroyed.

After the fire there was no real interest in rebuilding the community. Folsom, a mere two miles distant, was booming in 1856. Today only a marker on Green Valley Road serves to remind us that a place called Mormon Island ever existed.

Alabama Bar

One half mile below the forks of the American, on the south bank, is Alabama Bar. Today it marks the site of Folsom Dam. The bar was settled in 1850. However, not until the summer of 1852 did the Alabama Bar Mining Company begin the first mining at the site. Twelve men from Alabama named the bar, and the company at its peak employed up to 60 miners. Active mining continued for about four years at the bar until 1856 when the company was disbanded.

Beam's Bar

A half mile below Alabama Bar, on the south bank of the American where Folsom Prison now stands, is the site of Beam's Bar. Jerry Beam made his strike there in 1849, and his company of 12 miners was quite successful, averaging about a pound of gold per day per man. Beam sold out to a company headed by a man named Roland, but this new group of 12 worked the area for the next two years with little result.

In 1852 the bar was the scene of an attempted claim jump. Fourteen men led by a man named Schofield moved under cover of night to take over Roland's claim. A man named Johnson, one of Roland's men, was awakened by the jumpers and in the ensuing fight, one of the interlopers was fatally wounded. There was no prosecution, apparently because the Roland group made a liberal donation to the dead man's family.

Roland and his men abandoned the claim in 1857. No further attempt was made to mine Beam's Bar until 1862 when Alfred Spinks brought in a large workforce of Chinese, reported to be 120 strong. This group dug 60 feet to bedrock but found no gold.

Slate Bar

On the north side of the American, between Folsom Prison and the town of Folsom, is a ledge of solid granite called Slate Bar. The ledge permitted only what was called "crevice mining" – essentially what James Marshall did when he picked up the first flakes in the famous tailrace – and mining was not as extensive as on other bars. In 1850 James Smith built a store on the bar. He built a sawmill the following year. In 1852 Smith built a grist mill which he operated until 1854, when Edward Stockton purchased the site. An unsuccessful attempt to quarry granite at the site was made by Griffith Griffiths in 1856.

Mississippi Bar

Gold was found in 1849 at Mississippi Bar, on the north shore of the river (now the shore of Lake Natoma) opposite the present city of Folsom. The bar was said to have been named by a fur trader from Mississippi who had asked Sutter for suggestions on the best place to do business with Indians. It subsequently supported a few hundred miners during 1849-50 and was an important settlement for several years after. It was also the terminal point for an ambitious project to carry water from Tomarro Bar on the north fork of the American to the dry diggings downriver.

The American River Ditch extended 39 miles from the mountains to Sailor and Mississippi bars, where the water was returned to the river. This company numbered among its officers a prominent judge, A. P. Catlin, and A. T. Arrowsmith, an engineer who organized the Natoma Water Company in 1851.

A newspaper noted in 1879 that J. T. Cardwell had been severely stabbed "by Chinamen" while collecting taxes. The violent reaction by the Chinese was not customary; however, it was common practice of that time to discourage the Chinese from mining by the imposition of a "foreign miner's tax."

Gold mining accelerated with the advent of dredging operations that began at Mississippi Bar in 1899. In later years, a good part of the huge piles of boulders left by the dredging was crushed into gravel by Teichert Aggregates. When California State Parks was in the process of acquiring the worked-over area, the company did major earth-moving to create ponds and help prepare the site for park use. The area is now part of the Folsom Lake State Recreation Area.

Mississippi Bar, downstream from Folsom on the north side of the river, was a booming mining camp in the 1850s. It was later dredged into huge windrows of cobbles, but a portion has been rehabilitated as part of the State Park System, in an agreement with Teichert Aggregates, which operated a gravel plant in the area.

Sailor Bar

About a mile and a half below Mississippi Bar, also on the north side of the river, lies Sailor Bar, said to have been named for two sailors who had jumped ship to go prospecting and found gold there. Dredgers worked over much of the area at the turn of the century. It is now a county park and part of the American River Parkway.

Sacramento Bar

Sacramento Bar was described in mining days as "on a branch of the American River ditch, inside the bend of the American River, opposite Buffalo Creek." On today's maps, it is shown on the north side of the bend in the river opposite Lower Sunrise Regional Park.

Farmer's Diggings

This site was on the south side of the river, just below Sacramento Bar.

Ford's Bar

Located "on the lower American, below Farmer's Diggings," Ford's Bar is thought to have been a mining site, though Gudde notes that "no mining records were found." It would have been the farthest downriver of any gold mining site.

Negro Bar

The settlement of Negro Bar was on the south bank of the American River, adjacent to the present city of Folsom and across the river from the Negro Bar unit of Folsom Lake State Recreation Area. According to an annotation on an 1854 map by transcontinental railroad planner Theodore Judah, "Upwards of $2 million has been taken out of Negro Bar since 1849." (*Gudde*)

Long neglected, the site was largely obliterated by construction of Nimbus Dam in the 1950s. It suffered further with the construction there of an abutment of the Lake Natoma Crossing in 1990.

Discovered by "some colored gentlemen" in late 1849 or early 1850 (*Placer Times, Feb. 9, 1850*), Negro Bar may have been the first site discovered on the river by African Americans, a number of whom mined on the river, as evidenced by such place names as Negro Flat, Negro Hill, and Little Negro Hill.

At Negro Bar itself, however, it appears that few, if any, African Americans remained by the middle of 1850, as mining operations became more complex and large companies of miners took over.

Even the name changed to "Long Island Bar" (*Placer Times, May 8, 1850*), for the 38-member Long Island Mining Company, one such organization. The 30-member Tennessee Company was another.

Most ambitious was the 240-member Virginia Mining Company, which turned the entire river out of its channel there, in order to mine the exposed river bottom. The company worked the claim with little success for about two years, and then disbanded.

In a few years the settlement itself faded away, absorbed by the growing city of Folsom.

Texas Hill

Just below the Negro Bar-Folsom area, on the south bank of the river, was Texas Hill. This community maintained the post office for Negro Bar, Alder Creek, Natoma and Prairie City from November 1852 until it moved to Folsom in 1857. Texas Hill was an excellent source of the cobble stones used to pave the streets of San Francisco and to build the levees around Sacramento. In 1863 the Sacramento Valley Railroad bought up the land, however, and the community soon disappeared.

Ashland

This once-thriving community was founded as "Big Gulch" on the bluffs directly across the American from Folsom. The town was located on the route of the American River Ditch which passed through the settlement.

Around 1856 Big Gulch saw the arrival of a fascinating, fast-talking "promoter," one Colonel Russ. The colonel quickly won the hearts of the settlers who changed the name of the town from Big Gulch to Russville in his honor.

In the late 1850s while George Bromley was serving the old Sacramento-Folsom railway as train conductor, there came to Folsom a Colonel Russ who had made a fortune in New York City as a paving contractor.

Colonel Russ had invented a machine to cut granite and while at Folsom he conceived the idea that he could extract gold from the granite bluffs along the American River opposite Folsom. He was a very persuasive man and soon had a company organized with the purpose of mining the bluffs.

The company was known as the Russ Bluffs Gold Mining Concern, of which Colonel Russ was president and George Bromley secretary. They sold shares in the enterprise, which Bromley said "went like hot cakes."

Men were employed to sink a shaft on one of the high bluffs and they toiled industriously for several weeks. Then Bromley thought it was time for him to investigate the mine and see what prospects there were for gold.

He sent a statement of his conclusion to Colonel Russ and asked him to advertise a meeting of shareholders. He concluded that there was no gold in the bluffs and ordered the men to cease work.

At the meeting in Patterson's Hotel in Folsom, Bromley's announcement fell upon the happy crowd as a shock and bitter disappointment. But there was money enough in the treasury to meet all bills and pay for their dinner, so they felt a little better.

Then they solemnly voted to "dig carefully around the shaft, turn it upside down and sell it to the government as a lighthouse." (*Oakland Tribune*)

Russ wasn't discouraged. He next "invented" a wonderful machine that would plane the granite into blocks to be used in building "magnificent" structures in the valley. But Russ's new scheme met the same fate as his mine.

The eloquent and persuasive colonel, even after his two major failures, managed to get himself elected to local office. As justice of the peace, he demonstrated a unique flair for the office:

He put up a small flag pole and an elevated platform about six feet high, and when a case was to be tried, up went the stars and stripes on the flag pole and the Colonel mounted the seat of justice. Law statutes were of no use to him. He dispensed his own brand of justice. Any person asking for an appeal was immediately fined for contempt.

Russ finally lost both his money and his friends and left town. After the colonel's departure, the town was known for a short while as "Bowlesville" and in 1860 was renamed Ashland. By 1871, however, most of the citizens had moved across the river to Folsom.

Natoma Water Company and Prairie City

At the point where the American River flows from the foothills near Folsom, it forms a delta or "alluvial fan" which was rich in placer gold. Bluffs along the north bank of the river act as a natural barrier which forces the "fan" to form to the south. But without water to wash the gravels of the delta, the land was relatively worthless.

In 1851 miners at Mormon Island formed the Natoma Water Company to meet their increased need for water. The principal force among this group was A. P. Catlin, a '49er from Dutchess County, New York.

Catlin had been a prominent lawyer before coming West. He served in California's legislature and was appointed Superior Court Judge for Sacramento County. His most cel-

Prairie City was a social and economic center for the dry diggings southwest of Folsom. Today only a freeway ramp and a State historical marker attest to its existence.

ebrated achievement was securing Sacramento as the permanent seat of state government. He also successfully argued the Leidesdorff grant case before the U. S. Supreme Court in 1863. This was the landmark that finally settled land titles in the Folsom area.

The Natoma Water Company began work on a diversion dam near Salmon Falls on the South Fork of the American in 1852. In March of that year the company filed notice of its "intent to appropriate water by means of a canal" with the county recorder in Placerville. On July 31, 1853, in what was probably a move to gain more capital, the company reorganized as a joint stock company known as Natoma Water and Mining Company.

By mid-1853 the Natoma canal reached Prairie City. It can be said that the community was created by Natoma Water and Mining Company.

> Prairie City occupies a position on a portion of the plain of the Sacramento Valley, 25 miles from Sacramento City, and between the Placerville Coloma Roads.
>
> Gold was known to exist in the locality and to be scattered for miles over and near the surface of the earth, as early as 1850; but on account of the absence of water, could not be exhumed from the soil.
>
> In 1853 the Natoma Canal Company (sic) at great expense introduced the desirable element from the South Fork of the American River, conducting it by ditch and flume for a distance of 20 to 25 miles.
>
> From this period dated the growth of the prosperity of the village … Miners made a rush for the spot — having previously staked off their claims — and in the somewhat notorious phrase of the times, immediately "pitched in."
> (*Sacramento Record-Union*)

The cost of construction of the Natoma canal might have been prohibitive if the miners had not been willing to exchange labor for water. The Natoma flume across New York Ravine, for example, was 1,791 feet long, rose to 83 feet at its greatest height, and was constructed in three tiers costing $30,000 to build. When the flume was carrying its full capacity of water, it weighed 900 tons.

Business was good in Prairie City right from the start, especially since the town also served as the business center for the camps at Rhodes' Diggings and Willow Springs Hill. In the summer of 1853 two stages ran daily from Sacramento and there were already some 100 buildings erected. In 1854 the population reached 1,500 or even 2,000, according to the *Sacramento Pictorial Union*. In 1855 a steam powered quartz mill was constructed and in 1857 a French company spent $50,000 to erect a second mill.

As early as 1855, however, there were signs of decline:

> Without being famous for "large strikes" these mines (around Prairie City) have paid a regular and respectable percentage on labor.
> They have become a favorite resort of Chinamen, large numbers of whom have taken up their residence in the neighborhood and work the refuse portions of the ground with much assiduity. (*Pictorial Union*)

The presence of large numbers of Chinese miners was a sure sign of declining production, for Chinese were normally not welcome until white miners were sure an area had been mined out:

> Some days ago (December 1905) the *Union's* Folsom correspondent, in referring to the revival of mining in the vicinity of that place, told of the recent discovery of good diggings in the locality where once stood the thriving, bustling mining town of Prairie City in this country — a statement that brought back interesting memories of olden days to the few survivors in Sacramento and elsewhere of the time when the gulches and ravines in the eastern part of the county swarmed with gold diggers.
> Prairie City was located a few miles south of Folsom, on the road to Michigan Bar, but if any of the men who dug gold dust about there and who used to sell their dust in the busy town were to return after the lapse of fifty-five years ... it would puzzle them to point out the spot where Prairie City stood,

Chinese miners were usually relegated to already worked over claims but, by intensive labor, still made them pay.

with its streets, its stores and hotels, for there had not for many long years been a vestige of that place to be seen.

Instead of the red-shirted and high-booted miners, the only denizens of the gulch have been cows, jack rabbits and coyotes. Where the merchants at one time did thriving business, and the rattle of stage wheels was heard all the day through, the solitude is broken now only by the occasional cowbells, and the doleful nocturnal yelp of the coyote. (*Sacramento Union*)

Today nothing remains of the town that stood where Highway 50 crosses Prairie City Road, just south of Folsom.

Hydraulic Mining

In 1855 a new mining technique was devised that was massively destructive of the land: hydraulic mining. Ironically, it was the only totally new method developed during the Gold Rush. Operations were rather modest in the beginning, with nozzles about an inch in diameter directing a stream of water against a gravel bank. The run-off was channeled into sluices which collected gold in riffles, on the same principle as the rocker or long tom. Between 1855 and 1870, however, improvements were made in the equipment which revolutionized the industry. And in 1870 Richard Hoskins of Marysville began producing the "monitor," a water gun which literally blasted away entire mountainsides.

The monitor required water in huge quantities. In 1871 the State Surveyor General reported that 516 ditches with an aggregate length of 4,800 miles were in use, carrying water to the aqueous artillery.

With a rumble like thunder rolling close in the mountains, the giant monitor swung in a lowering arc, sending a stream of tortured water into the rubble of dirt and boulders, cascading a flow of mud and debris down into

Hydraulic mining washed great quantities of "slickens" into the river.

the sturdy riffle boxes and through a tunnel out of the hydraulic pit down
the precipitous chasm in whose bottom the American River glimmered.
(*Grass Valley-Nevada City Union*)

Destructive as hydraulic mining was, it was also profitable. One company using 2,000 "inches" of water (a miner's "inch" equals approximately 17,000 gallons of water over a 24-hour period) for 100 days, washed one million cubic yards of placer gavel and took out $32,000 worth of gold. Of this, $12,000 was clear profit.

By 1879 the number of ditches had increased to 640, with a total length of 6,585 miles. These ditches delivered a total of 260,000 "inches" of water each day, equivalent to almost two million gallons per day for every day of the year.

The miners recovered only the gold. There was no system for restraining the accompanying debris, called "slickens," from the mines. It washed down the stream beds into the valley rivers below. River beds rose, natural banks no longer contained the rivers, and the existence of Sacramento valley agriculture was threatened with suffocation under the huge mass of mining debris:

> The state engineer estimated from actual surveys in 1878 that 18,000 acres
> of valley land on the Yuba, once the choicest in the state, had been buried
> beneath mining debris. (Bancroft)

The American River was no exception. Although never affected to the same extent as the rivers and communities farther up the valley, it still was under the influence of hydraulic debris. In 1881 it was estimated that 20 million cubic yards of debris had been deposited in the bed of the North Fork.

As concern for the debris problem mounted, the Sacramento County Board of Supervisors decided to act. Their target was the Gold Run Ditch and Mining Company. A group of Sacramento men had formed the company in 1870 with a capital stock of $900,000. They had purchased unworked claims on the upper reaches of the North Fork of the American, built some 30 miles of ditches, and began hydraulic mining.

On July 30, 1881 Sheriff Ashley from Sacramento served an injunction at the Gold Run company headquarters in Dutch Flat. On November 15, 1881 the case came before Superior Court Judge Jackson Temple:

> Its importance ... rises to the highest plane, because it has brought to its
> management some of the best minds at the bar of California and an ex-Justice of
> the Supreme Court Bench, besides other attorneys of broad experience and high
> character at the bar.
>
> The presiding judge himself is an ex-Justice of the Supreme Court.
>
> As to the developments in the case, it is to be noted that no trial in
> California has ever brought forward such an array of talented engineers,
> chemists, physicians, and gentlemen of high scientific attainments. They have
> occupied the witness stand day after day, and (have) been subjected to the most
> searching and intricate of examinations.
>
> This case has brought forward also some of the most skilled and experi-
> enced agriculturists of the state ... (*Sacramento Record-Union*)

This case was before the court for seven months. Then on June 12, 1882, Judge Temple granted a permanent injunction prohibiting the company from depositing "coarse" debris in the American River:

The "Chinese Diggings" now within the Natoma Station development near Folsom, were a late form of hydraulic mining. This moss-grown trench once served as a sluice and also as a drain to carry the mining debris into the river.

I have concluded to so find that when the heavier debris is completely impounded, mining may be resumed, virtually refusing to hold that the plaintiff (Sacramento Board of Supervisors) may enjoin such operations as only corrupt the water with mud and render it less suitable for domestic and other uses.

Perhaps I am somewhat moved to this by the consideration that otherwise mining can never be prosecuted at all … I confess I shrink from the consequence so far-reaching. (*People* vs. *Gold Run Ditch and Mining Company*)

While not the total victory that they had hoped and expected, farmers rejoiced that they were able to enjoin the mining interests from using the river as an unrestricted dumping ground. As was to be expected, the company appealed Temple's decision to the state Supreme Court.

Before the Supreme Court completed its deliberations, a similar case was decided in a federal court — *Woodruff* vs. *North Bloomfield Gravel Mining Company*. The federal case took more than a year and a half to complete.

The miners were confident of a decision in their favor, for the judge hearing the case, Lorenzo Sawyer, had been a miner at Coloma. In the course of the hearing, Judge Sawyer made several trips to the mines and farms to see the situation for himself. Special commissioners questioned more than 200 witnesses and compiled 20,000 pages of testimony. Sawyer's opinion filled 225 pages and required three and a half hours to read. It amounted to a complete victory for valley agriculturists. Sawyer declared that dumping mining debris into the rivers was a public and private nuisance in both common and statutory law. Miners were perpetually enjoined from dumping any kind of debris, coarse or otherwise, into the rivers.

In late November 1884, the state Supreme Court upheld Temple's earlier decision in the Gold Run case, with one major exception. The decision to permit mining if coarse debris was kept from the rivers was reversed:

No person, natural or artificial, has the right directly or indirectly to cover his neighbor's land with mining debris.

As the *Grass Valley Tidings* mourned, "The last ray of hope of judicial relief" has vanished.

A stroke of judicial pen had stopped hydraulicking, but the debris remained. It continued to be a problem on the American River, where slickens continued to raise the river bed until 1896. After that year, the natural scouring power of the river was able to handle the lessening debris.

Chinese Diggings

A somewhat less damaging form of hydraulicking did continue into the 1900s. Called "ground sluicing," it is best exemplified by the "Chinese Diggings," a small part of which remain in a large private development at the northeast corner of the intersection of Highway 50 and Folsom Road.

With high pressure nozzles outlawed, miners used water propelled by gravity to wash the gold out. At the Chinese Diggings (the miners are presumed to have been Chinese) water was brought in along a ridge by the Natomas Company and allowed to wash down through a series of herringbone trenches into a main drain that also served as a sluice to remove the gold.

The drain, still largely intact in 2005, is only shoulder high, but as much as 30 feet deep at the lower end, where it enters the tunnel through which the debris passed under Folsom Road and into what is now Lake Natoma.

Gold Dredging

After the demise of hydraulicking, the next major technological advance was the gold-mining dredge. Although at least one dredge operated in California as early as 1850, dredging did not make its appearance along the American River until around 1900. The American River, or Folsom, District was one of the largest dredge fields in California, producing $125 million in gold, according to state estimates. It covered an area 10 miles long and up to 7 miles wide in places. The district extended from Folsom westward to the Rancho Cordova-Mather Field area, and embraced lands on both banks of the American River.

More than a dozen companies operated dredges along the Lower American River at such sites as Mississippi Bar, Sailor Bar and Negro Bar. A leading example was the Folsom Development Company, controlled by the Armour meat packing company. It operated six dredges beginning in 1904. Offices were maintained at Natoma (known then as "Dredge" because of its large dredge building and repair facilities,) consisted of shops, offices, a retort building and company-owned employee cottages. The Armour company used the color yellow extensively and those who lived in its housing were known as "Yellow Town Kids."

Gold dredges (back left) processed massive quantities of gold-bearing gravel as they worked over the old mining areas in the early 1900s

Natoma Vineyard entered the dredging business because of a disease, *phylloxera*, which attacked company vineyards. With the onslaught of this blight, the land became more valuable for mining than for agriculture.

During World War II gold production was curtailed by the government. Production resumed after the war but it was destined to be short-lived because available dredge land was depleted, and increased land values reduced the profit in dredging new sites. The last dredge, owned by the Natomas Company, ceased operations in 1962.

The following is a brief description of how a dredge operates:

> The standard placer mining dredge consists of a wooden hull with an opening, or well, in the center extending to the middle of the hull.
>
> A superstructure, or gantry, supports the upper end of a ladder and a line of buckets to excavate the gravel is mounted on this ladder, which may be lowered or raised.
>
> The buckets fill with gravel, the gravel is dumped into a hopper. From the hopper the gravel passes to a revolving or shaking screen which separates the coarse gravel from the fine. The coarse material passes over the screen and is stacked in piles behind the dredge.
>
> The gold bearing material passes through perforations in the screen into a distributor and then over a series of riffle sluices or gold-saving tables on which mercury is sprinkled to amalgamate and save the gold. (Lewis Aubry, *Gold Dredging in California* State Mining Bureau, 1910)

Periodically the dredge was shut down and the gold-quicksilver amalgam in the gold-saving tables recovered. The amalgam was taken to a retort house and subjected to a complex refining process to separate out the gold, which was then melted and formed into ingots.

Some of the dredgers had no actual gold aboard, only amalgam. They had little to fear from high-graders or thieves. Only one such attempt has been recorded:

> Stories of wealth-collecting abilities of the dredges apparently reached the ears of one ambitious robber who, under the cover of night, boarded one of the huge clanking boats.
>
> Suddenly striking a menacing stance in the center of the dredge, he ordered the crew to break out the gold, not knowing the recovered gold accumulated in a locked area inaccessible even to the operating crew.
>
> At the "hands up" order one quick-thinking dredge man threw the main switch, plunging the boat into total darkness.
>
> The robber, in strange surroundings anyway, was terrified at being in the center of that huge machinery where one false move could mean a horrible death by mangling.
>
> As soon as his eye could locate the dim outline of an opening, he made a dash for it and disappeared into the night, thus ending in dismal failure his ill-conceived plan for the first (and probably the last) great dredge robbery in the history of mining. (Jack R. Wagner, *Gold Mines of California*)

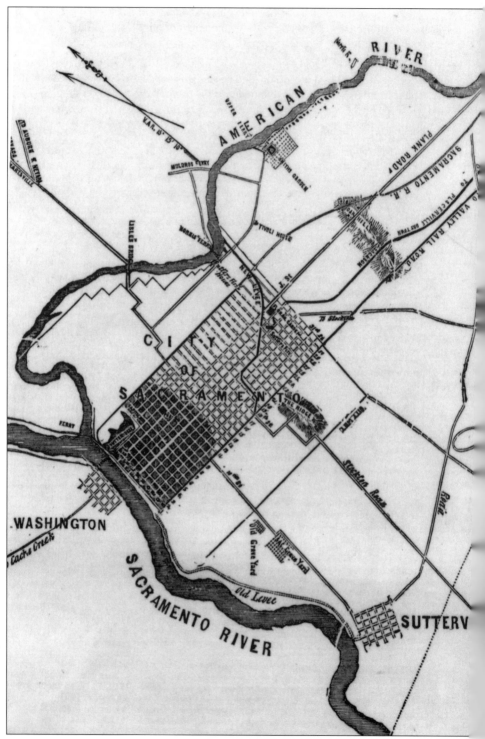

Map of Sacramento and vicinity, 1855, shows early transportation routes.

Chapter 5

Transportation

In the eyes of the station keeper and the hostler, the stage driver was a hero — a great and shining dignitary, the world's favorite son, the envy of the people, the observed of the nations.
— Mark Twain, 1871

The American River provided a natural transportation route between Sacramento City and the Sierra Nevada. Travelers, whether miners, merchants or settlers, used the trails, roads and the railroad which paralleled the river to reach their destinations. There was even some travel on the river itself, although this was limited by its shallow depth.

The earliest travel routes along the banks of the American were Maidu Indian trails. Sutter and other early settlers found these trails to be ready-made and convenient means of communication between their ranchos. Sutter's workmen and early settlers followed a route along the river to reach the sawmill site at Coloma.

Thus by the time gold was discovered, the route along the American River to the gold fields was already well-established. Miners walked and rode along this route, possibly stopping along the way to try their luck panning in the river on their way to the Mother Lode. A road was established by the constant flow of traffic out of Sacramento City along M Street to Brighton on the south side of the river. From Brighton, several roads to the gold fields branched out, including the Jackson Road (modern Highway 16), Coloma Road, Folsom Road, and the Placerville Road (modern Highway 50).

Ferries, Bridges, And Roads

Because these roads were on the south bank, miners heading for the northern mines and those who lived or grazed stock on the north bank needed a convenient way to cross the river. According to the reminiscences of Thomas S. Bayley:

> Previous to 1850 nearly all the travel to the northern mines crossed the American River at the ford four miles from the city at what was called Norris' Ranch … In the early spring of 1850 the waters were very high, and a ferry boat was indispensable (sic).
> My father A.S. Bayley, on a trip to Coloma halted a few hours at Brighton, and the subject of a ferry came up. A resident of the place said that he had a scow on the river and travelers were continually troubling him to set them across the river, that he would like to sell the boat, so as to be relieved of the trouble and vexation, did not think it would pay much anyway. He offered the boat to my

father for $500 and he need not pay for it until he made it out of the business.

My father thought that it would pay well if moved down to the old ford and put into operation. He bought the boat, came on to Coloma and I went back with him to take charge of his boat. It was moved down the river and a couple of Kanakas employed to put a cable across the stream and get the scow in position.

The boat was pulled across the river hand-over-hand. The fees for the ferry service were $1.50 for a person on foot, $4 for a person and horse during the day, or $8 at night.

Bayley remembered an amusing story about some of his regular passengers:

At that time, Capt. Childs had possession of the Norris Ranch and resided there on the north side of the river with his family of three girls about grown. In an indirect way they were quite a benefit to the ferry. Several young (or middle-aged) men would come out from the city every Saturday and Sunday night on horseback. The residence was immediately on the bank of the river. But it would be beneath their dignity to leave their horses and cross afoot, as they always came after dark, and returned that night. Their ferry bill was $16 each.

Bayley's Ferry, being on the Coloma Road, appears to have been the one ferry shown on a rough map drawn by General Riley after his visit to Sutter's Fort and the mining regions in July 1849. It was probably also the ferry that the ever expansive Sutter was referring to when he told people "his" ferry was so busy it couldn't handle all the traffic coming to it.

After 1850, the ferry changed hands several times, first becoming Sinclair's Ferry and finally Norris' Ferry, also known as Upper Ferry.

Rancher Samuel Norris also established a bridge there in the 1850s, which after withstanding several large floods washed out in the great flood of January 1862, when the river rose a record 60 feet.

Bridges

Another ferry established in 1849 was Sam Brannan's ferry at Mormon Island. It was replaced by a bridge in 1852, known as "Shaw's Bridge" after the bridge operator. It also washed out in '62.

To compete with the Mormon Island bridge and draw people and trade to the town of Negro Bar (soon to become Folsom), Abraham G. Kinsey in 1855 built a wooden bridge about 300 feet upstream from the present Rainbow Bridge. Six years later, the California Central Railroad built its bridge, also at the Rainbow Bridge site.[1]

Kinsey's bridge was swept away by flood waters in March 1857, but by June stages were already crossing its replacement, a higher and stronger wire suspension bridge. Nonetheless, this too was carried away in the 1862 flood, when the only bridge left standing on the river was the 92-foot high California Central Bridge.

Undaunted, Kinsey and a partner built yet another bridge, 16 feet higher than the last. Though battered by floods, it stayed in service until it was finally condemned in 1890. Two years later, on a quiet night in May, the old bridge collapsed "with an earth-shattering crash" after one of its main cables gave way, apparently cut by pranksters.

---

[1] The California Central's first passenger train ran over this bridge from Folsom to Lincoln in October 1861. Plans called for the line to be extended to Marysville, but this never came about. In a short while the new Central Pacific Railroad took over the California Central and tore up its tracks. Around 1867, the bridge, no longer maintained, collapsed into the river.

The County, which had acquired the bridge in 1880, replaced it in 1893 with a 370 foot steel arch bridge, the longest single-span bridge on the Pacific Coast at that time. It was also the river's first two-way bridge, wide enough for wagons to pass one another. In 25 years or so, however, this bridge too declined to the point at which it had to be condemned, to be replaced by the Rainbow Bridge.

Downriver, at the foot of today's 16th Street, a Mr. Turner operated a ferry from the Fall of 1849 through the Spring of 1850. At the time, the site was known as "The Lower Ford" and his ferry as "The Lower Ferry," until that name was usurped by a ferry at the mouth of the river established in June 1850 by Thomas Rucker and James C. Davis.

In 1850, Daniel Lisle took over the operation and installed a steam-powered ferry to replace the hand-operated one. In 1851 he went on to build a bridge at the same location – required to be a draw bridge so steamboats could go upstream as far as Sutter's Fort. (cover)

The bridge was described by *Gleason's Pictorial* in 1852 as "the most substantial bridge of its kind in California, being 620 feet long, 25 feet wide, and standing 30 feet above the low water mark." All stages for Marysville, Nevada City, and Auburn used it, the magazine reported. Lisle also persuaded the Board of Supervisors to maintain the road leading from the bridge to the "Let Up and Jingle House" on the Auburn Road as a public highway, further encouraging travel over his bridge.

Lisle operated both the toll bridge and ferry until 1860, when he drowned while working on his ferry. Time after time the wooden bridge was severely damaged by winter floods, then patched and damaged again, until it was replaced in 1864. Still plagued by floods, the second bridge was itself replaced in 1888 by a still more substantial County-operated bridge, which lasted into the following century.

The Rucker and Davis ferry, which crossed the mouth of the river at 2nd Street, continued under various ownerships until purchased in 1860 by Judge C. H. Swift, who continued to operate it while building a bridge. The bridge was 500 feet from bank to bank, and 17 feet wide. It was built on 10" pilings 40 feet long, shipped down from Puget

Lisle's Bridge over the American River in 1852. It was about where the 16th street bridge now crosses.

Sound, and Swift, though luckier than Lisle, almost lost his own life when his boat capsized while he was supervising the pile-driving.

Swift's bridge washed out in the March 1861 flood, but by July a new bridge had been built a few yards below. This span was floated on barges and was connected to the banks with a gangway. It was constructed with funds collected by ranchers on the north side of the river who had constant business in Sacramento and wanted a free bridge across the river. A temporary structure not expected to withstand high water, it washed away during the winter floods of 1861-62.

Another ferry, known as the "Middle Ferry" was established in May 1850 near the end of today's 28th Street by William Muldrow. After lengthy legal feuding, Muldrow became a partner of Samuel Norris, operator of the ferry and bridge at Brighton, for the purpose of building a toll bridge at the 28th Street site.

The two bridges though badly damaged, survived a major flood in 1861, but were destroyed by the historic flood of 1862. The 28th St. bridge withstood the raging waters for two days, but on a stormy Saturday afternoon, with a crowd of spectators tensely watching, two huge sections broke away, smashing into the north bank of the river a short distance downstream. Parts of the bridge were still floating in June.

Only the Lisle Bridge was rebuilt, and in 1894 it was reported that the only other bridge was the Central Pacific Bridge a mile and a half above Lisle's Bridge (where the 16th Street Bridge is now).

Roads

The early roads along the American River were poorly maintained. Riding on roads such as the one out M Street to Brighton must have been an uncomfortable experience, judging by the report of His Royal Highness Duke Paul Wilhelm of Wurttemberg after a visit to Sacramento in 1850. Governor Peter Burnett invited the Duke to attend the Fourth of July celebration at Brighton as his guest. The Duke, Governor Burnett, the Vice Governor and John Sutter led the procession out to the picnic grounds in a four-in-hand

Sacramento in 1853 was the headquarters of James Birch's California Stage Company, which provided transportation along the American River.

In 1897, Folsom Road was chosen to be made the model highway for California's proposed state highway system, according to historian C. Raymond Clar. The project was never carried out, but in 1910, when the highway system did finally come into being, Folsom Road was included as one of the first units.

carriage pulled by "four handsome, spirited white horses." The Duke gave the following description of the scenery and ride as they left the city and entered the country:

> From now on we could see trees along the banks of the American River. They were tall and beautiful, the only greenery in sight. At this time, however, it (the river) had a scant depth of some two or three feet. With no regard for the ruts and frequent holes, often quite deep, and for ditches that crossed the road, a grave danger and extreme discomfort to the passengers, we plunged ahead in a frenzied haste as far as Fort Sutter … The procession then moved on again, until we arrived at Brighton. .

The M Street route was not the only easterly road out of the city. Due to the heavy flooding during the winter of 1852-53, a toll plank road was built from Sutter's Fort along an extension of J Street to Brighton and the Patterson House. The object of this road was to provide a road that would be free of mud and dust year around. The road failed as a business venture, however, because teamsters saw no need to use the toll road during the dry season when they could drive along the flat river plain for free. The road could not survive on just flood-time fees.

Freight Wagons

Eager miners and settlers were not the only early day users of these roads. Freight was transported along this route from Sacramento City to Folsom where it was dispersed among the northern California mining communities. Later in the 1850s and 1860s freight was carried over the mountains to Nevada.

When the state failed to fund a road across the Sierra, Sacramento went into partnership with Placer and Yolo counties. They built a road from Placerville to Lake Tahoe 12 feet wide, cleared of brush and rocks, along the South Fork of the American River close to present-day Highway 50. In a stroke of fortune, it opened just in time for the discovery of silver in Nevada.

After a few years, there were so many people on the road that it was often difficult for wagons to get back in line after a turnoff and early traffic jams could limit progress to a few miles a day. The first big success of the Central Pacific Railroad was not a railroad, but a dirt highway the company built on the railroad's planned route. That provided a road through Auburn along the North Fork of the American River near today's Interstate 80. Wagon drivers liked the Auburn road best and the tolls they paid provided badly needed cash to build the railroad.

At the beginning of the gold rush, there were no wagon roads much farther than the outskirts of Sacramento. Even after the main roads were built to Auburn and Placerville, there were still hundreds of mining towns that only tough little mules could reach. But each mule could carry 300 pounds almost anywhere. Thousands of mules averaged 30 miles a day on steep mountain trails, carrying everything from whiskey and flour to chairs and plows. They used a soft, straw-stuffed leather pack saddle that the Mexicans invented. It was a big improvement for the animals over the wooden crossbucks the Americans used and soon the U.S. Army adopted the Mexican system.

At first, freight was hauled on recycled emigrant wagons brought down from Oregon after crossing the plains. They were too light for hauling freight, and craftsmen began designing their own type of wagons, some of which could carry up to 15 tons. With a trailer, big wagons could haul as much as a modern truck. Since every miner needed at least a pound of goods a day, moving supplies was a major business — hundreds of teams left Sacramento for the mines every day. In 1852 some 137,000 tons of goods worth $8,000,000 ($144,000,000 today) were shipped out of Sacramento. In 1856 a traveler passed 82 teams, all heavily loaded, between Sacramento and Placerville — an average of one every half mile.

Stage Coaches

Even for the early 49ers, stage service was provided between Sacramento and the gold fields. James Birch arrived in Sacramento from Rhode Island in the summer of 1849 with a coach for his own stage line. His first route began at Sacramento and ended at Coloma. Only two years before, the 50-mile road that the stage followed had been a pack trail following the American River up into the mountains.

Only a year after Birch started, there were several lines running regularly out of Sacramento. In two more years there were 12 companies, each with an average of eight coaches and 100 horses. In addition to carrying passengers and delivering supplies, coach companies carried gold from the mines They were called stage coaches because they often operated in stages of about 100 miles a day, usually stopping at night so their cramped occupants could have some bed rest. But not always: the run from Sacramento to Shasta was straight through — 30 hours of bouncing over 188 miles of potholes and rocks. Stage drivers made few attempts to avoid bumps, choosing instead to let the horses pick their way down the road so the team could find its way at night or in fog.

There were hundreds of stage robberies and with a few famous exceptions, stage robbers were rarely caught. One of those exceptions was gang leader "Rattlesnake Dick" Barter who, after a lengthy, fruitless effort to find gold on Rattlesnake Bar on the North Fork of the American, turned to robbery, cattle rustling, and stealing from miners' sluice boxes. His career ended in a hail of bullets from a sheriff's posse near Auburn in 1859.

Stagecoaches peaked during the late 1850s, although stages continued to operate until 1915. Even though trains took over some main routes, stage lines still covered all the towns off the train lines from railway terminals such as Folsom, Auburn, Lincoln and Newcastle.

Wells Fargo

Wells Fargo owned stages and other wagons to move mail, gold and supplies all over the west. Its first office can be seen in Old Sacramento today. By the late 1850s, the company had branches all over the gold country where people picked up mail, deposited gold and money, and shipped packages. Today's Wells Fargo Bank is a direct descendant of that early institution that began in San Francisco and Sacramento.

Pony Express

The Pony Express moved express mail by non-stop horse relays across the west between Sacramento and Missouri in 10 days. Starting from Sacramento at 2:45 a.m., April 4, 1860, rider Sam (Bill) Hamilton carried the first mail of the Central Overland Pony Express eastward. Ahead were remount stations, roughly along the Lower American River, at 5 Mile House (at California State University), 15 Mile House, four miles east of Mills (Rancho Cordova) on White Rock Road, and Folsom, Sutter Street near Decatur.

Several months later Folsom was made the western terminus, and the Sacramento Valley Railroad carried the mail between Folsom and Sacramento.

The beginning of the Pony Express route is marked by a statue on Second Street in Old Sacramento.

The Pony Express kept communications opened to California at the beginning of the Civil War and proved that determined men could move across the country even in winter. This helped give people courage to build the transcontinental railroad. The Pony Express shut down with the coming of the overland telegraph in 1861.

Good Roads Movement

Except for the privately built and operated toll roads, roads were a county responsibility; the Folsom Road was declared a public highway by the Sacramento County Board of Supervisors on June 6, 1859.

Auto stages eventually replaced the horse.

A movement began in the 1890s to improve the roads of Sacramento County. Farm, business and bicycle groups enthusiastically supported the project. A Good Roads Convention in September, 1893 recommended that the State of California establish a highway commission, and by 1895 statewide agitation finally resulted in the Bureau of Highways. Its first report proposed the road that is now Highway 50.

A great deal of bureaucratic maneuvering resulted in the postponement of the creation of a state highway system until 1910. The Bureau of Highways was replaced by the Department of Highways in April, 1897 and then renamed the Highway Commission in March 1909.

In 1907, a Sacramento County Highway Commission was given the task of coordinating the expenditure of $825,000 for roads countywide. A macadam surface was applied to the main thoroughfares and new bridges were built in strategic places.

20th Century Bridges

The Twentieth Century ushered in a new era of bridge building across the American River to handle increased traffic resulting from the development of suburban Sacramento, Carmichael and Fair Oaks on the north bank. By the end of the century, 21 bridges spanned the river between its mouth and Folsom Dam, with at least two others planned.

One of the more recent crossings materialized in 2000 when the city of Folsom welcomed "The Little Bridge That Came Home." This was Folsom's 1893 steel truss bridge that had stood unused as traffic poured over the newer Rainbow Bridge. In 1931 it was dismantled and moved 200 miles to span the Klamath River in far northern California. More than 100 years after it was built, it was no longer needed on the Klamath. But Folsom needed a bicycle bridge, so it was taken apart and moved back to Folsom and carefully set on the same piers on which it had originally stood, just upstream from the Rainbow Bridge. Named the Folsom Historic Truss Bridge, it is used by hikers, cyclists and horseback riders on the trail at the east end of Lake Natoma.

At Folsom, the Rainbow Bridge, admired as the only arch-style bridge in Sacramento County, was completed in 1925. Built on the site of the old California Central Railroad Bridge, it succeeded five earlier bridges in the same area.

Nor did its construction end bridge building there. In 2000, a second bridge, called the Lake Natoma Crossing, was built a short distance downstream at Negro Bar. The project went forward over objections by supporters of Folsom Power House State Historic Park, who felt the south abutment was too close to the historic power house, and friends of the Negro Bar unit of Folsom State Recreation Area, who opposed construction of the bridge across Lake Natoma and through State Park lands on its north shore.

A third bridge was scheduled for completion by 2007, this one just below Folsom Dam to relieve congestion caused when the road across the dam was closed as a security measure following the 9/11/01 terrorist attacks in New York and Washington D.C.

About five miles downstream, below Nimbus Dam, another bridge crosses the river at Hazel Avenue. Built by Sacramento County in 1966, it was designed primarily for vehicular traffic. But it also has a special railed-off lane connecting the end of the riding and hiking trail on the south bank of the river with the trail's continuation along the north shore of Lake Natoma.

Some 2½ miles farther down the river is a complex of bridges serving a variety of users. The Fair Oaks Bridge, a suspension bridge built in 1908, is the oldest. Closed to traffic after the new Sunrise Avenue Bridge was built a short distance downstream in 1964, the old bridge became the property of the Sacramento County Parks and Recreation Department (now the Regional Parks, Recreation, and Open Space Department) and in 1973 the department re-decked and painted it, then reopened it, but only for use by pedestrians, bicyclists, and horseback riders.

Between the two bridges, a low level bridge originally built for gravel hauling has also been acquired by the County Parks Department. Named the Jim Jones Bridge in honor of a longtime leader of the Save the American River Association and a founder of the American River Parkway Foundation, the bridge serves bikers, fishermen, photographers, and other summertime visitors.

A bit farther down the river is the Harold Richey Memorial Bicycle Bridge, connecting the Jed Smith trail between William Pond Recreation Area on the north side of the river with the trail's continuation in Goethe Regional Park on the south bank. It's also popular with a variety of users, including walkers, sightseers, and occasionally even people with horses.

The next bridge downstream is the Watt Avenue Bridge, built by the County in 1959, with later improvements culminating in widening it to six lanes with attractive artistic decoration along walkways in 2004. A short distance downstream at Howe Avenue, another bridge was built to help relieve congestion on the Watt Avenue Bridge and the venerable H Street Bridge, about a mile farther down the river..

Built in 1911, the H Street Bridge was replaced in 1932, and has undergone a number of improvements since, in efforts to keep up with ever increasing traffic.

Halfway between the last two bridges stands a miniature Golden Gate Bridge. A bicycle and pedestrian bridge, it was designed and painted to mimic the San Francisco landmark. Built in 1967 and named after Guy West, first president of Sacramento State University, it provides access to the campus for students and others living on the north side of the river.

About 2½ miles below the H Street Bridge, the Capital City Freeway crosses the river. And just below the freeway bridge is the Union Pacific Railroad Bridge, on a site where trains bound for the Sierra and beyond have crossed the river since the location was picked for the Central Pacific Railroad by Theodore Judah in 1867.

Below this are two other railroad bridges. First is the Western Pacific Railroad Bridge, opposite 20th Street, built in 1906 and currently used by Union Pacific. A short distance beyond is a 1907 bridge built to carry the third-rail interurban trains of the Northern Electric Railroad (later the Sacramento Northern), which served cities in the upper Sacramento Valley. Abandoned when the railroad ceased operation, it has since been converted to serve bicyclists and pedestrians.

At the 16th Street site of the old Lisle Bridge, a new bridge now carries Highway 160 traffic out of Sacramento. Incoming traffic crosses on another bridge, at 12th Street, and parallel to that is a new Rapid Transit railroad bridge.

Near the mouth of the river is the Interstate 5 Bridge, built in 1968. Close by, another bridge is planned for rapid transit trains en route to Sacramento International Airport.

The last bridge before the American joins the Sacramento River is the old Jibboom Street Bridge. Jibboom Street was named for the forest of jibs and booms of the Gold

The Capital City Wheelmen, here crossing the Fair Oaks Bridge, were early proponents of a bicycle trail from Sacramento to Folsom.

Rush sailing ships that docked near it. Built by the County in 1929 to link the City of Sacramento with the Garden Highway, it is now used to provide access to Discovery Park. The only drawbridge on the America River, it was made part of the State Highway System in 1957, but returned to the county when the I-5 Bridge was built.

First Bike Path

Roads have served the recreational needs of the Sacramento community as well as purely functional ones. The Capital City Wheelmen used the American River and the roads along it for recreational purposes as early as 1886.

Since they did not have a good road on which to ride, the Wheelmen voted in March 1896 to build a cinder path to Folsom. They began building an experimental path from 31st and J Streets out to the levee near Brighton Junction. This section of the path was successful, so the club began to make plans to extend the route to Folsom. Each member was assessed $1 and Sacramento merchants and citizens donated $900. Contributors received a "Patron of the Wheelway, C. C. W." ribbon. The first permanent section was completed as far as Brighton in April 1896, and on April 12 some 500 cyclists rode the new path. A second section was completed to Alder Creek, but funds began to run out. Folsom merchants came to the rescue, and the path was completed to Folsom.

The path was officially designated the C. C. Wheelmen Bikeway. The County Board of Supervisors banned other vehicles from using this trail. However, farmers found it convenient to use the cinder path during the muddy winters, so parts of the path had to be replaced with decomposed granite. With the new surface, a new speed record of one hour and 2 minutes replaced the old mark of one hour and 40 minutes between Sacramento and Folsom.

In 1973, the American River Parkway trail system was designated the "Jedediah Smith Memorial Trail" by the Sacramento County Board of Supervisors. The impetus for the project was a $100,000 bequest by Charles M. Goethe, local philanthropist, naturalist, and history buff. Goethe had asked that the money go toward a trail along the river honoring Smith who, in 1827, was the first American to travel along the river as he and his small party of fur trappers sought a pass over the mountains.

The word "memorial" was included in the name to indicate that the parkway trail was an approximation of the actual route of Smith and his men, since it has never been precisely identified. The trail has since been designated a National Recreational Trail.

Goethe's bequest was used to enlarge and extend the parkway and its trail system. It was appropriate that a bicycle trail would be a major feature, as Goethe among his many activities, had been an enthusiastic member of the Capital City Wheelmen as a youth. Public support for the trail widened in an era in which famed heart physician Dr. Paul Dudley White urged regular exercise, especially by bike-riding, for health's sake. A Bikeway Action Committee, Sacramento Region, organized by Elmer Aldrich and other State Parks employees, helped win support from local governments for a systemized plan of developing local bikeways, including on the parkway. Federal Judge Thomas MacBride was a vigorous supporter of a parkway bike trail.

Harold Richey Memorial Bicycle Bridge

The bicycle and pedestrian bridge spanning the river from William Pond Recreation Area in Carmichael to C. M. Goethe Regional Park in Rancho Cordova was named the Harold M. Richey Bicycle Bridge in memory of a man known to many as "Mr. Bike Trail."

He was not only instrumental in the establishment of the trail but for years afterwards served as the trail's unofficial watchdog to insure the preservation of its integrity. He was also renowned for his encyclopedic knowledge of the trail, its history, and its surroundings.

Richey had taken up bicycling after a heart attack at age 60, in order to "recondition his heart." From then on, he could be found on the trail almost daily until his death in 1986 at the age of 81.

The bridge, built in 1979 with funding from a local park bond act, has been a vital piece of the trail system, providing a long-wanted connecting link between the bike trail on the north side of the river from Discovery Park to William Pond Recreation Area and the trail on the south side running eastward from Goethe Park, a route often followed by Richey as he watched for any incursions on the parkway that might endanger the trail.

River Transport

Transportation on the American River itself was unreliable. The navigability of the river was closely tied to the seasons. During winter flood times steamers could make their way as far as 12 miles upstream, but during the dry summers, low water stopped them from passing Brighton near present day CSUS. Even under the best conditions, however, only vessels with shallow drafts could be used.

The first recorded use of the American River as a navigable waterway by non-Indians was in August 1839. John Sutter traveled a few miles upstream from the river's mouth and landed near present-day 28th Street.

On April 20, 1850 the then navigability of the American River was demonstrated. The *Placer Times* ran the story:

> A company of ladies and gentlemen assembled onboard the *Etna*, a new steamboat of ten-horsepower on Wednesday last, and enjoyed an excursion up the Rio do los Americanos to Norristown, it being the occasion of opening communication through this channel with the above point. Owing to the machinery propelling for the first time the youthful stranger in strange waters, there was noticeably some degree of timidity in its performance, and perhaps it lessened the esteem in which the boat was held against the current of general thought — for all on the *Etna* appeared to think there was no danger of eruption … The boat is owned by Captain Gelston, who in person dispensed the ginger pop and refreshments …

A few weeks later a sailing vessel ventured up the American River. Again Gelston captained the vessel. The *Daily Alta California* said:

> We had the pleasure yesterday of a delightful ride out along the banks of the American River to the site of a new town. It is situated on that locality known as Brighton. We had the gratification of seeing also the arrival at Brighton of the first sailing vessel that ever navigated this stream. To Capt. Gelston belongs the credit of having sailed the first vessel of heavy tonnage up the Rio Sacramento, the first steamboat up the American River, and now the first sailing vessel up this important branch of the Sacramento … This vessel that arrived there is called the *Curlew*.

When the flood of December 1852-January 1853 forced many Sacramentans to move upstream to high ground, vessels traveled beyond present-day California State University, Sacramento to the temporary town of Hoboken, on the south side of the American River. The *Democratic State Journal* reported on an "Excursion to Hoboken:"

> The establishment, by many of our merchants, of trading stations on the

high grounds along the American River at Brighton and elsewhere has proved a measure of larger profit to them ... We took occasion to visit these places on Saturday, ascending the American on board the small steamer *R. K. Page* ... Her course was slow and laborious and attended with some danger from the numerous snags now concealed in great part by the height of the water. Numerous barges, scows, etc., enlivened the river at short intervals, and were propelled by all the various methods applicable to such voyaging ...

Sketchy reports state that vessels went up the river as far as Texas Hill, near Folsom. For several years the trade was large in cobblestones gathered along the American River in this vicinity. The stones were used to build levees and also to pave streets in San Francisco. Prior to the completion of the Sacramento Valley Railroad, these stones are said to have been loaded into scows and taken to Sacramento and transferred to schooners to San Francisco.

With the increase in hydraulic mining, navigation became more difficult on many of the Central Valley rivers. Sand bars began to build up in river channels, making travel by large vessels more difficult. In 1859 it was reported that slickens from the hydraulic mining had created a sand bar across the mouth of the American and stopped most navigation at that point.

During the flood of 1861-62, however, the river was sufficiently high for large vessels to go farther up the American River than ever before recorded. On January 11, Captain Gibson and the steamer *Defiance* left Sacramento for an excursion up the American:

> She passed Lisle's Bridge — carried away by the recent floods — and reached a point a little below Norris' Bridge. While in sight of this structure it (the bridge) yielded to the force of the flood, and a portion of it was carried off. The *Defiance* took from various houses on the river near Rabel's tannery and Burn's slough some five women and fifteen children and brought them to the city.

The next day the *Defiance* again started up the American River, this time with 40 passengers and 60 tons of freight destined for Folsom. The Sacramento Valley Railroad track between Sacramento and Patterson's had washed out in spots in the flood, and steamer connections were the only way to maintain communications with Folsom. By evening the *Defiance* had reached Patterson's, 12 miles up river, 7 miles farther than any streamer had ever been. At Patterson's it met the train from Folsom. The steamer then took on 100 passengers bound for Sacramento. The *Governor Dana* also left Patterson's loaded with 75 tons of freight.

One purpose of these flood excursions was to pick out a spot for a temporary embarcadero east of Sacramento — a second Hoboken. By the beginning of February a location had been found about a quarter of a mile above Hoboken and five miles from the mouth of the American. This temporary flood-time town was named Mitchville, in honor of McMitchell, a freight agent for the Steam Navigation Company. The town consisted of only a few buildings, including a steamboat office.

For about a week the steamer *Sam Soule* made a trip twice daily to Mitchville carrying freight. But by February 7 the *Sam Soule* was making only one trip a day, and the water had fallen so low that it touched a bar a short distance below Lisle's Bridge.

The last large steam vessel to travel up the American was the 80-foot steamer *Daisy*, which made trips between Sacramento and Folsom in the spring of 1882. Her job was to bring down cobblestones and firewood. Because she could not clear the 12th Street

Bridge, she had to be hauled ashore and winched overland around the bridge. On the return trip her barges were released above the bridge and picked up by another vessel for the remainder of the journey.

Apparently the *Daisy's* passengers were sometimes rowdy. A local newspaper reported that "It was a jolly lot only for Folsom, but for a right royal time." A *Record-Union* reporter on board the *Daisy* sent back this message:

> All right up to this time. We expect to reach Folsom sometime before next Christmas. The crew and passengers are well supplied with roast pig, chickens, and bread and butter. We don't expect to starve before December 26th.

Later on the same trip the *Daisy* ran aground near Mississippi Bar.

The *Daisy's* owner, J. T. Cardwell, was a speculator in the firewood business. He kept his wood piled along the north bank of the river near present-day Carmichael and wanted to use the *Daisy* to transport it downstream. But in August 1882 the woodpile was apparently set afire. Cardwell became discouraged and gave up his attempts at navigating the American River and sold the *Daisy* to a fishing company in San Francisco.

The legal head of navigation on the American River has changed several times over the years. The earliest state declaration on the subject set the head of navigation at a place referred to in the Statutes of 1850 as "the place called mill dam at the head of the race made by Captain J. A. Sutter for the erection of a grist mill." This was approximately nine miles upstream from the river's mouth. State research shows that the site of the grist mill dam was at the westerly edge of the Rancho de los Americanos.

In 1851 the point of legal head of navigation was changed to the town of Brighton. By 1853 it was again changed to Lower Ford, a few roads above Lisle's Bridge at 12th Street. These and successive statutes placed the upstream limit of the river nearer and nearer to its confluence with the Sacramento, until in 1860 the river was omitted entirely from the statute listing the state's navigable rivers.

Railroads

Railroads solved several basic problems in transportation to the mines and mountain communities. While navigation on the American River was unreliable and road transportation was slow and often impossible during the muddy winters, transportation by rail was reliable, fast and relatively inexpensive.

The first major operating railroad west of the Mississippi was the Sacramento Valley Railroad (SVRR). The SVRR came into being in October 1853 when Colonel Charles Lincoln Wilson filed the Article of Incorporation with the State of California. Wilson envisioned a railroad linking Sacramento with Negro Bar and Marysville, two of the most important mining supply distribution centers in the northern part of the state.

Wilson contracted with the firm of Robinson, Seymour and Company to lay the 40 miles of track. Building costs were expected to be about $1,800,000 or $45,000 per mile. Pioche and Bayerque, a San Francisco banking firm, became the financiers and the controlling interest in the railroad. Other San Francisco financiers involved with the project were Commodore C. K. Garrison, an early San Francisco mayor; Captain Joseph L. Folsom; William T. Sherman, an 1850s banker and later Civil War general; and Ralph S. Fretz, partner of banker William C. Ralston.

Construction on the right-of-way began in February 1855. Chief Engineer Theodore

Dehone Judah surveyed two preliminary routes that went eastward out of Sacramento. One followed an extension of M Street, the other followed R Street. The R Street route was chosen since it did not cut through as much private property. The gauge of this railroad was set at five feet.

Work progressed well until June, with the rolling stock already being delivered to Sacramento. Then financial problems began to tie up the project. The dry winter had led to gold panic, and the stock of the SVRR was forfeited for nonpayment of assessments. Colonel Wilson lost much of his own money when the bank that held his funds failed. Appeals for money went out to those financiers who still had cash, but to no avail. The contract with the construction company had to be changed, eliminating the costly stretch between Negro Bar and Marysville. On August 10, 1855 Colonel Wilson was replaced as president of the railroad by Commodore Cornelius K. Garrison. William Tecumseh Sherman, whose bank remained solvent, became vice president.

One of the first railroad trips west of the Rockies occurred when civil engineer Theodore Judah, who later became the tireless advocate of the transcontinental railroad, and three others placed a handcar on the short stretch of the newly laid rails on R Street in Sacramento on August 11. A week later the SVRR's first locomotive, the *Sacramento*, arrived on the schooner *Two Brothers*. It had traveled from Boston via Cape Horn to Sacramento. The day after the *Sacramento* arrival, Lester Robinson of Robinson Seymour and Company invited 200 guests for a short trip on the new track. The participants were treated to a grand excursion to 17th Street.

By October 1855 the rails were nearing Negro Bar, and three more locomotives had

The "Pioneer" was one of the first locomotives of the Sacramento Valley Railroad.

been added. The *Nevada*, companion engine of the *Sacramento*, arrived from Boston and the *L. L. Robinson* arrived from New Jersey. Commodore Garrison brought up the *Elephant*, the first locomotive in the West, from San Francisco where it had been used to level sand dunes. The locomotive was renamed the *C. K. Garrison*.

At Christmas the tracks nearly reached Folsom, the new town just above Negro Bar that Judah had surveyed. The route passed through Brighton, Patterson's, Salsbury and Alder Creek. A gala celebration officially opened the railroad on Washington's Birthday, 1856. Special trains ran to Folsom, with over one thousand people enjoying the Railroad Ball held at Meredith's Hotel.

The SVRR ran two trains daily from Sacramento and two from Folsom. The fare for the trip between Sacramento and Folsom was $2. The toll for freight shipped from Sacramento to Folsom was $8 per ton. The toll for the return trip was only $2.25, because cargo shipped from Folsom to Sacramento consisted mainly of bulk shipments of granite, cobblestone and grain.

In a ten-month time span in 1856, the railroad carried 550 tons of granite, 360 of which were used in Sacramento with the rest shipped to San Francisco. As an added source of profit, the railroad contracted 20 of its cars to haul 140 cords of wood from Alder Creek and Salsbury Station. This wood was sold for $6.50 a cord in Sacramento and $8.75 a cord in San Francisco.

By 1856, even though the SVRR was doing a good business, the company still suffered from financial problems, and the railroad ownership had to be reorganized under the trusteeship of J. Mora and Moss.

A year later, in June of 1858, ground was broken for the tracks of a new railroad, the California Central. Charles Lincoln Wilson, the first president of the SVRR, was the major organizer of the new company. He planned to finish what the SVRR had started, and build on from Folsom to Marysville. But investment capital for railroad projects was scarce, and when the company began operations in 1861, there were tracks only between Folsom and Lincoln, where California Central's offices were located. The company used SVRR cars pulled by their own locomotives.

The California Central Railroad connected with the SVRR at Folsom. The section of its right-of-way near Folsom had proven to be costly; it consisted of two heavy cuts on either side of the American River, a high bridge over the river, a 50-foot approach trestle on each side of the bridge; 45 feet of trestling across Big Gulch Ravine; 55 feet across China Ravine; and a cut through China Hill, about a mile below Russville, which was 40 feet deep and almost entirely through decayed granite and cemented gravel. The bridge was located near the present highway bridge over the river at Folsom. Modern-day Greenback Lane follows the railroad right-of-way just north of the river.

The railroad bridge was a 213-foot-long span that was approached on either side by wooden trestles. The 209-foot arc under the bridge was intended to support the 300-ton main bridge as well as its own 150 tons. The top of the main bridge was 100 feet above the river bed, and it was the only bridge on the American River to survive the 1862 flood. It lasted until 1867 when it collapsed into the river with a thunderous roar. By that time the California Central from Folsom to Roseville had been abandoned because of its absorption into the Central Pacific.

New Railroads

In April 1862 yet another railroad began operation. The Sacramento, Placer and Nevada Railroad was incorporated to tap traffic passing thorough Auburn to the northern mines. It, too, began as a grandiose scheme to build eastward to the mining and lumber districts of California and Nevada. The SP&N contracted with the SVRR to supply all the locomotives and cars on its tracks, which connected with the California Central tracks just north of Folsom at Ashland (Russville). The SP&N's main westbound freight shipments consisted of copper ore from the Home Copper Mines Company in El Dorado County and granite from the Wildwood Quarry owned by Griffith and Company in Placer County. The Wildwood Quarry provided granite for the building of Fort Point in San Francisco.

Like most early California railroads the company financially fell short of its goal. It only reached a point five or six miles short of Auburn, near Newcastle. When the Central Pacific reached Newcastle, it took control of freight in that area. The SP&N went bankrupt and was sold at a sheriff's sale in 1864.

SVRR forces, attempting to compete with the Central Pacific Railroad building eastward, removed the SP&N track and used it in the construction of the SVRR extension from Folsom to Placerville, called the Sacramento and Placerville Railroad. Major confrontations occurred when the Central Pacific people, in an attempt to slow the construction of this new railroad, obtained court injunctions to stop the removal of the old SP&N rail.

Eventually the track was removed, and the Sacramento and Placerville Railroad extended its lines from Folsom to the new town of Latrobe in October 1864 and to Shingle Springs the next June. The conflict ended in August 1865 when the members of the Big Four — C. P. Huntington, Charles Crocker, Leland Stanford and Mark Hopkins — bought out the stockholders of SVRR, which owned the Placerville extension, for $800,000. The SVRR was operated as a separate railroad until consolidated as part of the Southern Pacific on April 19, 1877.

Central Pacific

On June 28, 1861 the Central Pacific Railroad Company of California was organized by the Big Four and other financiers under the general incorporation laws of the state. Theodore Judah, the company's chief engineer, after making preliminary surveys over the Sierra Nevada, was sent to Washington, D. C. to lobby for legislation to provide them with financial aid. The result was the Pacific Railroad Act of 1862 which provided land and money to the company as incentive for construction. This act of Congress also specified that the gauge for the transcontinental railroad be 4 feet by 8½ inches, unlike earlier wider tracks.

Groundbreaking ceremonies for the railroad were held January 8, 1863 at the foot of K Street in Sacramento. The first rails arrived in Sacramento on October 8, and the first locomotive on November 10 of that year.

Construction of the Central Pacific Bridge across the American River was begun in December, 1862 and finished in the fall of the next year. The bridge was four miles east of Sacramento by rail and was the longest bridge and trestling on the Central Pacific between Sacramento and Promontory. The line of trestling was 2,200 feet long on the south side of the river and 615 feet on the north. The bridge crossed the river in two spans of 192 feet each, and was six feet above the highest water level known up to that time. The total length of the main structure was 397 feet, and it contained 188,000 board feet of lumber. It weighed 400 tons and could support a load of 375 tons. By December 4, 1863, rail had already been laid one mile beyond the bridge.

The bridge burned in 1867 and was quickly replaced by another wooden structure. A steel span was later built to replace the wooden bridge. This steel bridge later fell into the river, taking a loaded train with it. The present steel span dates from 1912.

Two other railroads crossed the American River at Sacramento, the Western Pacific and the Northern Electric (later Sacramento Northern). The Sacramento division of the Northern Electric, a third rail electric interurban, was built southward to Sacramento in 1907. The Western Pacific, the last of the transcontinental railroads to be built, began in Oakland in January, 1906 and reached Keddie, California where it met track from the east in November, 1909. Its track, like that of the Northern Electric, crossed the American River a little above the Twelfth Street Bridge. Both bridges exist today, but the Northern Electric bridge no longer carries rails, but is part of the bicycle trail. It also carries a city water main to North Sacramento.

Chapter 6

Controlling The River

When the water began to rush in and overwhelmed the place, there was
no adequate means of escape for life and property, and consequently
some were drowned in their beds and many died in consequence of the
terrible exposures to which they were subjected ...
— *Dr. John F. Morse, diary entry, 1850 Sacramento flood*

Early settlers in Sacramento City and in the surrounding county eastward to Folsom saw the American River as a force to be reckoned with. Charging down out of the snow-clad mountains, it often overran its banks, especially during mid-winter and early spring. And thus would end the hopes and dreams and even the lives of many, including one man who was wearing a money belt and when his small boat sank and he could not save his gold and himself, apparently chose to go down with his riches.

Conversely, there were days of drought when the river was so low that people could walk across it. But even after the dams went up in the mid-1950s, there would not be enough water in the face of growing demands. And hard-pressed water managers imposed "minimum flows" of Lower American water — often a life-or-death matter for tiny Chinook Salmon eggs and other natural resources along the river and its parkway. Thus did fickle nature tease humans who lived near the river.

Floods

It rained heavily during December and January, 1850, and both the Sacramento and American Rivers rose rapidly, until finally on Jan. 8 the City of Sacramento flooded. Communication between Sacramento and the mining region to the east was cut off by the first major flood in historic times. Others followed in 1852, 1853, 1861, 1862, 1867, and 1878.

John Sutter had recognized the damage that river overflow could cause and urged the settlers to build their town on slightly higher land at a place he called Sutterville, near what is now William Land Park in Sacramento. Instead they chose to settle at the spot with the greatest potential for flooding: where the rivers come together. Sutter knew enough to build his fort on higher ground, at today's 27th and K streets.

The 1850 flood trapped a young Swiss merchant, Theophile de Rutte, on the top shelf of his store. In his "Adventures of a Young Swiss in California," he wrote:

> ...tired of waiting and calling out, I resigned myself to spending a second
> night in company with the rats that seemed to be feasting on their sacks of

flour. I follow suit and started to nibble on a few biscuits, but the fever had dulled my hunger.

Besides, I was suffering more from a lack of water than of food. To bring up water, all I had to do by then was to stretch out my arm, the level having risen about thirteen inches during the day so that it was only two and a half feet from me.

… If at daybreak the danger of being submerged had not passed, I had decided to break through the roof by attempting to raise one or two boards with my head, and then to straddle the peak and call and scream until a passerby might come and get me.

—Theophile de Rutte, 1850

De Rutte told of witnessing a "strange spectacle:"

American Fork had carried and deposited everywhere in its path a gold-bearing silt of little value it is true, but sufficiently rich to attract the attention of the city's inhabitants. Soon the entire population was transformed into as many miners, and everyone sought to procure for himself a dish, plate or cup to pan this silt, which fortunately for businesses in danger of being abandoned, was paying from a day's washing a maximum of only two dollars, so that the Americans, little satisfied with such a small amount, wasted no time in returning to their usual occupations.

"The city is one vast lake and boats are busily engaged in passing to and fro, conveying people in search of meals and lodging," wrote *The Sacramento Bee* in a "Flood Sheet" published while its own building was under water.

American Samuel Norris saw the 1850 flood situation as an opportunity to establish a new town near the present site of the California State University, Sacramento, campus. In April, Norris claimed that it was free from floods and was a good site for the distribution of goods for the mines. However, Norristown remained a paper city only. The citizens of Sacramento City were more sympathetic towards building a better levee system around their already established town than spending money to develop a new town on a site with poor port facilities.

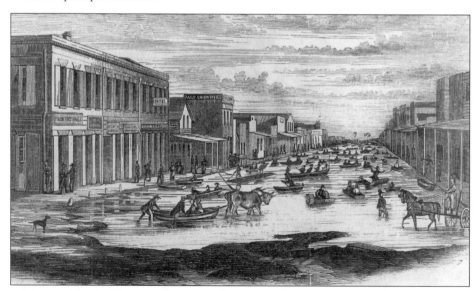

Devastating floods frequently inundated Sacramento in the early days. You needed a boat to cross J Street during the flood of December 1852.

After the unhappy experience of 1850, Sacramentans began erecting levees around the city. However, during the early spring of 1852 continuous rains in the lowlands and heavy snows in the mountains caused a sudden rise in the American River. This resulted in a break in the levee near the mouth of the river shortly after midnight on March 7. People tried to close the break with dirt, bags, of grain and timber. But the flows increased and the bridge across China Slough at 3rd Street was swept away. The American River overflowed its banks above Sacramento and its waters churned toward the city.

Another major flood occurred the following Dec. 31. Both Sacramento City and the area to the east of it were flooded, thus cutting off trade with the mountains. Teams and pack trains could come no closer than nine miles to the city's eastside.

Hoboken

Again, as in 1850, a new town developed on the American River — this one called Hoboken. The site was one mile east of the town of Brighton, near the present CSUS campus. Hoboken was established early in January, 1853 and existed for six weeks as a supply depot for the mountain communities. Seventy Sacramento merchants set up branch stores. Four steamboats made daily round trips from Sacramento's embarcadero carrying merchandise to Hoboken where it could be sold and shipped out to the mines. Business was apparently brisk, for Hoboken merchants shipped $80,000 in gold to Sacramento City after two weeks in business.

Approximately 1,000 people made Hoboken their home throughout the duration of the 1853 flood. They even elected a mayor, who injected a bit of humor into their predicament. Speaking to the citizens of Hoboken he said, "You are an infant municipality … in a little while, a few sunshining days, and you will dry up." He was right — by Feb. 14 the roads into Sacramento had opened and Hoboken was no more.

Nine years later, Sacramento County residents were hit by four major American River floods during December and January, 1861-62. On December 9, 1861 the levees to the

The town of Hoboken sprang up on the river, near the present CSUS campus, to serve briefly as a shipping point when the 1862 flood cut off the railroad to Folsom and the mines.

K Street, looking East, during the 1862 flood.

east of Sacramento gave way and the river flooded the city. Lisle's Bridge over the American River near 12th Street was swept away. The river overflowed it banks also at Brighton. Water spread southward to the Sacramento Valley Railroad and washed away its superstructure and tracks. The railroad was passable only from Folsom to a point about one mile west of Brighton. Two weeks later, on December 23, while work was proceeding to repair Sacramento levees, the water rose again and inundated the city.

The flooding that occurred on Jan. 9-10 was worst of all. By this time Sacramentans were becoming rather fatalistic about these watery onslaughts. The *Sacramento Daily Union* announced unemotionally:

"Our city was visited yesterday by another destructive flood … "

At Folsom, the water rose 60 feet above normal, sweeping away the flour mill of Stockton and Coover and the newer one of Carroll and Moore. Also destroyed were the wire suspension bridge of Kinsey and Thompson, and indeed, every other bridge on the American River between Folsom and Sacramento except the California Central Railroad bridge at Folsom.

Indian people living near Marysville left their homes and went up into the foothills one week before the disastrous Jan. 9-10 flood. Predicting an extraordinary flood, they told the whites it would be higher than it had been for 30 years.

Because of the high water, steamers were able to go farther up the American River than ever before. Some of this activity ceased, however, when the steamer *Gem* was carried through the break at Rabel's Tannery in late January and hit high ground in an orchard near 23rd and B Streets. By Feb. 3 the Steam Navigation Company was making arrangements to remove the *Gem* to dry land using hydraulic house-raising apparatus. On Feb. 21 the *Gem* was moved to the river's edge and re-launched.

Mitchville

Rail and road connections between Sacramento and Brighton were flooded out. Mitchville, a temporary depot, was founded.

On February 3, 1862 the *Sacramento Daily Union* printed a description of this new business community.

Mitchville — This is the name of a new town located on the American River, about five miles from its mouth and about a quarter of a mile above the point which Hoboken was situated in 1852. The town is named in honor of McMitchell, one of the freight agents of the Steam Navigation Company, and consists of a frame of steamboat office, two whiskey ships, and an additional one for storage of freight. It is to this point that the steamer *Sam Soule* now makes trips, twice a day, carrying a large amount of freight, which is taken by teams to the Sacramento Valley Railroad, and thence distributed throughout the mining region supplied from this portion of the State. The town presents a primitive appearance, and the indications are that it will not, for a few years at least, outrival Sacramento, to which it owes it origins. The artistic portion of the town consists of two signs, one of which is inscribed "Steamboat Office N B — No boarders taken here," and on the other the name of the town, "Mitchville." On the latter are two distressed looking gentlemen partaking of foaming lager, and another depicting an entirely naked hombre, whose appearance would excite sympathy from the most obdurate of our species. The latter picture is supposed to be, in measure, indicative of the accommodations afforded by the newly created city. We have no doubt, however, that the town will answer the temporary purpose for which it was called into being, and trust that it will prove profitable to all connected with it.

Several days later the paper reported that business remained lively at Mitchville. Several new businesses had opened their doors, including the grocers Daly and Rust, and two or three bars. Freighting was big business also, with as many as 40 teams waiting for the arrival of a steamer.

While the worst of the flooding was over, the American River levee gave way again at Rabel's Tannery on Jan. 22. A crevice 150 feet wide opened and the rush of water increased the gap to 800 feet. By Feb. 10, however, the water was so low in the American River that it had nearly ceased to run into the city through the break at Rabel's.

Because of this disastrous flood, the river near Sacramento was straightened to eliminate the curve near the tannery. The engineer for Swamp Land District No. 2 completed a survey of the river from Sacramento to the highlands at Brighton. He made the following report:

> Descending from the summit of the Sierra Nevada with a fall from 500 to 600 feet per mile, confined by canons from 2,000 to 600 feet in height, gathering in its descent the accumulating waters of gulch, stream, and cataract, the American river pours the drainage of more that 1,300 square miles of mountain area through the canons at Folsom into Sacramento valley, with a torrent velocity due to a fall of 6,000 feet in seventy-five miles, in the form of a crashing muttering wave, carrying destruction to everything moveable.

This report reinforced what many knew from practical experience. A great deal of water with a great deal of force was hitting the levee at the bend near Rabel's Tannery. People realized that it was senseless to attempt to build a stronger levee, and instead advocated construction of a new channel for the river.

An existing slough that cut across the bend was cleared and deepened to create the new channel. Engineer A. R. Jackson specified that the contractors would:

> ... clear off and excavate ... a space of 200 feet in width running across the bend opposite Rabel's Tannery. This strip of ground commences at a point opposite Twentieth Street, and is about ¾ of a mile in length.

Work began in August, 1862 but wasn't completed until Dec. 9, 1868.

At the same time another part of the river was straightened also. In its natural state, the river flowed to Sutter or China Slough (a few hundred feet from the river's mouth) and then into the Sacramento River. This caused much flooding within the city. However, a minor slough, at the point where the river entered Sutter Slough, also connected the American River and the Sacramento. This slough was deepened and became the new main channel of the American River. The former channel through Sutter Slough was blocked off and reclaimed by 1905.

Sacramento Rises

Meanwhile, Sacramento community leaders had come to the painful conclusion that to survive in the city's present location at the low confluence of two powerful rivers, it must literally raise itself. Thus was undertaken the mammoth, 15-year task of raising downtown streets, sidewalks and buildings as high as 10 feet. Streets were high-graded with wagonloads of fill from excavations to rechannel the American River. Dozens of men with jack screws raised buildings. Merchants were saddled with $200,000 in assessments and the expense of raising storefronts. And pedestrians were forced to navigate up-and-down sidewalks linked by rickety steps.

"At the height of this activity, Sacramento was described as a city on stilts," author

Thor Severson writes in *Sacramento: An Illustrated History*, 1839 to 1874.

But completion of the stupendous task refuted an earlier out-of-town editorialist's prediction that "Sacramento is a doomed city," deflated hopes of Hoboken and others to grab business advantage of Sacramento's flood problems, and quieted talk of moving the State Capitol elsewhere.

Reclamation

After 1862 people along the American River began to realize they could control the river and not remain its helpless victims. With the emergence of agriculture in the Sacramento Valley, a concern developed for the reclamation of the swamp lands that flooded annually. Land owners were worried about levee protection for their farms, elimination of the debris from hydraulic mining and the development of irrigation. But it was not until after 1900 that large reclamation projects were carried out because of the large amount of capital required. From 1850 to 1900 most of the overflowed lands were reclaimed piecemeal by individual farmers and communities.

California's two million acres of overflowed lands were acquired by the federal government in 1848 when it gained possession of the land from Mexico. Congress then ceded these lands back to the state in 1850 with passage of the Swamp Land Act (also known as the Arkansas Act), which required that profits from the sale of these lands be used for their reclamation.

According to the first regulations regarding the sale of swamp and overflowed lands, an individual could buy a maximum of 320 acres for a price of one dollar per acre, and take up to five years to pay the full price. By the end of five years, half of the land had to be reclaimed. In 1858 the law was amended so that an individual could buy a maximum of 640 acres, with no more than a half mile frontage on a navigable stream.

In 1861, the Legislature created a board of Swamp Land Commissioners. The board was authorized upon the petition of the owners of one-third of any tract of land susceptible to one system of reclamation to appoint an engineer to make a survey and plan for reclamation of the land. Two of these swamp land districts bordered on the American River.

The 1861-62 flood was not directly mentioned in the reports of the swamp land commissioners. However, their reports now recognized that the cost of reclaiming Districts 1 and 2 would be greater than the amount of their reclamation funds, an indication that the plans for the levee height had been revised due to the new high water mark set by the flood of 1862. There is no evidence that engineers for the districts had made any measurements or estimates of the quantity of water to be cared for, or of the capacity of the river channels. They apparently assumed that higher levee construction was all that was necessary to control the river. However, even this basic levee work was sporadic throughout the rest of the century.

The County Boards of Supervisors were authorized to create reclamation districts whenever the owners of more than one-half the land involved petitioned for one.

One problem encountered in these early reclamation projects was how to move dirt quickly, cheaply and efficiently. A solution was found in 1879 with the introduction of the floating clamshell dredge. This apparatus was a bucket swung at the end of a long boom and powered by a steam engine. Each bucket consisted of two jaws with iron teeth. This type of dredge could pick up fill from the river, drain the soil as it moved along and then deposit it on the riverbank.

Levees

An ironic situation developed as reclamation projects progressed. Levees were built to both help reclaim swamp lands and to protect from river flood water. At the same time, hydraulic mining upstream sent silt and debris down the river, filling up the stream beds so they could hold less water. When rivers rose during periods of heavy rain or snowmelt there was no place for the excess water or silt to run off. This created a two-fold problem: flood waters were channeled by a "canal" effect with a great deal of pressure, in the absence of natural flood plains, and silt was forced by the levees to stay within the stream beds, again in the absence of natural flood plains.

With reclamation projects and mining debris, the level of flood waters got progressively higher, leading to disastrous floods in Sacramento Valley in 1862, 1867, 1875 and 1878. Each flood brought a period of more levee building. The snowmelt of May 1867 caused the American River to rise to such heights that it flowed across the Sacramento into Yolo County north of the town of Washington. One engineering report stated that the American River is in reality of equal if not greater moment than either of the other streams, so far as public welfare is concerned; for while a large part of the Yuba and Bear Rivers' sands does find a resting place upon the plains and bottom lands, about all the American River detritus is found in the main river of the valley, at a most important point in its course.

The dual problem of flooding and mining debris reached such proportions that the Office of State Engineer was created in 1878. The first engineer was William Hammond Hall or, as he usually signed his reports, Wm Ham Hall. Due to the passage of the "Act to Promote Drainage," the State Engineer was charged with investigating the formation of drainage districts, to prepare plans and specifications for the works and to supervise construction.

Huge clamshell dredges built levees along the river to reclaim land and hold back the periodic flooding.

As recently as 1955, the river rampaged through much of Sacramento. At the H Street Bridge, flood waters spread out on both sides of the river and into the hop fields where Campus Commons now stands.

Reclamation began on a large scale after 1900. At that time large sources of capital like the Natomas Company were available for such projects. In 1911 District 1000 was organized in Sacramento and Sutter Counties, including the north bank of the American River near its mouth. The District was composed of more than 55,000 acres in the Beatty, Bennett, Central Elkhorn, Goodland, Meister and Riverside irrigation districts.

Central Valley Project

In the years after World War I concern turned from merely controlling the river to putting its water to use.

The Central Valley Project, of which Folsom Dam is part, began taking shape during the 1920s after drought economically hurt the farmers of the Central Valley. Based on proposals in the State Water Plan of 1931, the Central Valley Project was supported by farmers and pushed through the 1933 Legislature. A $170 million bond proposition was endorsed by California voters, but the bonds were not sold due to the Depression.

Instead, the federal government was called on for financial aid from President Franklin Roosevelt's public works program, and the Central Valley Project became a federal undertaking. In the decade since its beginning the Project has boasted that it has:

> circled the great valley with a necklace of majestic dams, wedged into the canyons of the Sierra and Coast Range. Primarily, the spacious reservoirs they have created are intended to hold runoff waters from the mountains surrounding the valley during the winter and spring and by dint of engineering marvels, drop these waters to the valley floor in measured installments during the hot summer months. The dams do other things besides. They prevent floods; they convert billions of tons of tamed torrents into electrical energy; they provide water to homes and industries . . .

Development of the American River at the Folsom Dam site was first officially mentioned when President Ulysses S. Grant sent the "Alexander Report," an Army Engineers document, to Congress in 1874. But no actual development took place until the 1890s when the California Gas and Electric Company constructed California's first hydroelectric project at the site.

The State Water Project included a proposal for a 355,000 acre-foot reservoir at Folsom, and the 1944 Flood Control Act authorized the Corps of Engineers to construct a control reservoir of that size. To meet the needs of a growing population, however, Congress authorized a larger 1 million acre-foot multi-purpose dam and reservoir with a 162,000-kilowatt power plant, along with a regulating dam and power plant downstream at Nimbus.

Folsom Dam was built by the Corps of Engineers, and the Bureau of Reclamation built the Folsom power plant, Nimbus Dam and Nimbus power plant. Upon completion Folsom Dam became the responsibility of the Bureau of Reclamation.

One of the honored guests at the 1948 groundbreaking was Norman B. Livermore, Sr. His grandfather, Horatio Gates Livermore, directed the building of the first American River dam at Salmon Falls in 1852. His father, Horatio P. Livermore, was a prime mover in the hydroelectric-power dam completed at Folsom in 1893.

Construction of the present Folsom Dam and power plant was completed in 1956 at a cost of less than $60 million. The structure is 1,400 feet long, topped by a 30-foot wide road that was closed for security reason following the 9/11/2001 attacks. Its maximum height above the lowest point in the foundation is 340 feet.

Storage of water behind Folsom Dam began in spring 1955. The storage capability and flood control features of the dam were tested in the historic flood of December, 1955. General William Cassidy of the Corps of Engineers stated that the dam saved Californians $180 million in damages. The damage that did occur added up to $150 million. The dam was tested again in 1964 by the failure of Hell Hole Dam on the Rubicon River upstream from Folsom.

Then came the record flood of February, 1986 when 10 inches of rain fell on Sacramento in 11 straight days. It dumped more water into Folsom than the dam is designed to handle, inflicted widespread damage on low-lying neighborhoods and sent the Lower American lapping to within inches of the tops of levees.

In 1995, a broken spillway gate in Folsom Dam drained half of Folsom Lake, washing out part of the American River Bike trail. Another near flood struck in 1997.

Just below Folsom Dam is Nimbus Dam. It was built in 1955 to regulate the flow of the American River through the Folsom power plant and generate additional power through its own power plant. Nimbus Dam serves also to direct water into Folsom South Canal and as a forebay for the Nimbus generators.

Nimbus Dam is 1100 feet long, including the powerhouse, and is 52 feet high from stream bed to crest. It has 18 steel radial gates measuring 24 x 40 feet. The dam's reservoir, Lake Natoma, extends about five miles upstream to a point near the Rainbow Bridge in Folsom. The total cost of the dam was $7,156,000.

The U. S. Bureau of Reclamation regulates the flow of the American River at Folsom Dam, which was completed in 1955 as part of the Central Valley Project.

The electrical output from the power plant goes to the Folsom switchyard and then to the Folsom-Elverta switchyard where it joins the Central Valley Project distribution network. The cost of the Folsom switchyard was $170 million, and the cost of the power plant was $4,199,000.

Folsom Dam was thought to have adequate storage for both flood control and downstream uses when it was constructed. But with the tremendous growth of the Sacramento Area, and new findings on the area's vulnerability to floods, this is no longer the case as was proven in the 11-day storm in 1986.

The river's salmon and steelhead and other fish and wildlife resources have suffered particularly because of inadequate flows released during their critical spawning and nursery periods.

While an additional dam above Folsom in the Auburn area was under consideration, it faced strong opposition by many political and environmental leaders who said it would be too expensive and too damaging to wildlife, plant and recreational resources of the river.

The Save the American River Association and others take the position that sufficient water is available, even in dry years, if the water releases are managed to serve all uses, including fish and other wildlife and recreation. The U. S. Bureau of Reclamation has been asked to restudy its existing water contracts with this in mind.

But the flood threat was of continuing concern to city and county leaders, especially when a U. S. Army Corps of Engineers study indicated that much of the metropolitan area could be inundated in a "200 year" flood, one that would be expected to have a 0.5 percent chance of occurring in any given year. After lengthy debate, Congress approved legislation in 2004 that would raise Folsom Dam by seven feet to increase capacity to Folsom lake, add new and larger flood gates to the face of the dam, and strengthen American River levees. By 2005 the Sacramento Area Flood Control Agency had completed raising or strengthening about 85 percent of Lower American levees scheduled and providing protection against a 100-year flood, or one with a 1 percent chance of occurring in any given year.

Water Shortages

Controlling the behavior of the Lower American River is a two-way street. Not only must it be harnessed to protect a densely-populated community against devastating floods, but it must be carefully managed in time of drought to help meet agriculture, municipal and wildlife needs, as well as providing flows to limit salt water intrusion in the Delta.

After completion of construction of Folsom Dam in 1956, the State Water Resources Control Board (SWRCB) established a minimum flow of 250 cubic feet per second (cfs) from the dam to the confluence of the Sacramento for the period from January 1 through September 14 and 500 cfs for the rest of the year. By 1969 it was evident to the Save the American River Association, fishing clubs and other environmental groups that such flows were inadequate for protecting the salmon and steelhead fishery and the intricate web of plants, animals and insects that lived on the American River Parkway.

In 1972, on the premise that the proposed Auburn Dam would be built, the State Water Resources Control Board established higher minimum flows to benefit fish and wildlife resources of the Parkway. From Nimbus Dam to the confluence, the flow would be 1,250 cfs from October to July 14. And to meet recreational needs from May 15 to October 14, a minimum flow of 1,500 cfs was established, except for dry years.

These flow requirements would not apply, however, unless Auburn Dam was built. And fisheries biologists subsequently concluded that even the improvements made by the 1972 decision would not adequately protect the American River fisheries.

The Folsom-South Canal posed another threat to the Lower American River, for it would take American River water from above Nimbus Dam. The long-range Bureau of Reclamation plan was to move water via the Folsom-South Canal south along the east side of the Central Valley. The Folsom-South Canal was only completed as far south as to serve the Sacramento Municipal Utility District's nuclear power plant at Rancho Seco, since de-activated.

Completion beyond that point has been blocked by a lawsuit filed by the Save the American River Association and the Natural Resources Defense Council. They felt such a diversion could seriously reduce the amount of water available to flow down the lower American. Also Auburn Dam, which was to provide water from its reservoir, was not built; therefore the water was simply not there.

EBMUD Decision

In 1970, the East Bay Municipal Utility District contracted with the U.S. Bureau of Reclamation for delivery of up to 150,000 acre feet annually (AFA) from the American River via the Folsom-South Canal for delivery to Oakland and other East Bay customers. This water was originally to come from Auburn Reservoir. The EBMUD-Bureau of Reclamation contract touched off a decades-long struggle by local environmental and governmental units who charged that such a diversion would harm Lower American River fishery, wildlife, recreation and domestic water supply values. In 1972, SARA, the Environmental Defense Fund, and the County of Sacramento sued to force the utility to take its water after it had flowed unhindered past the Parkway.

After years of appeals to state courts and the U.S. Supreme Court, Alameda County Superior Court Judge Richard Hodge upheld in a 1989 landmark decision EBMUD's contractual rights to American River Water. However, the decision significantly restricted EBMUD's diversions to protect significant public trust interests in the river such as its fishery and the riparian vegetation of the Parkway. In essence, the Hodge decision was a physical solution. Judge Hodge first established stream flow conditions and the timing of the flows from testimony presented by State and Federal fish conservation agencies that would be protective of the fish, other aquatic resources and ecological conditions of the Lower American River. It was only after these conditions could be met could EBMUD divert water.

Judge Hodge set minimum flows much higher than those set by the 1972 decision. He also left the door open to modify those restrictions pending studies to determine temperature and flow conditions necessary to protect adult salmon, tiny salmon eggs, and fingerlings of Chinook salmon and steelhead.

The ruling set forth for the first time flow requirements that many biologists agreed may be sufficient to protect the Lower American River fisheries. However, they applied only to EBMUD and not to other diverters nor to the Bureau of Reclamation, which controls all releases of American River water from Folsom Reservoir. For the Bureau, the flows in D-893 (1958 SWRCB decision), though inadequate to protect Chinook salmon and steelhead, still applied.

While EBMUD had been prevented from taking American River water through the Folsom-South Canal, steadily increasing local and statewide population growth added pressure for taking American River water. Such action led to creation in 1994 of an umbrella group dedicated to protecting the integrity of the Lower American River. The group, known as the Regional Water Forum, was sponsored by the Sacramento City-County Office of Water Planning and included environmental, business, building, agricultural, water district and community groups.

The Water Forum facilitated creation of a "Joint Project" by EBMUD and Sacramento City and County for the purpose of finding a non-Nimbus point of diversion for taking American River water. Negotiations stalled in 1998. Two years later at the urging of Sen. Dianne Feinstein, D-CA, talks on the project resumed. Such talks led to formulation of a plan for a Sacramento River diversion to be located at Freeport.

If given final approval, the Freeport facility would pipe water eastward to a new water treatment plant serving central Sacramento County before linking up with the Folsom South Canal. From there it would be carried south to tie in with EBMUD facilities carrying Mokelumne River water. The purpose is to provide EBMUD with a dry year water supply and emergency supplies.

Many public officials hailed this prospective truce in the longstanding "American River water wars" between Sacramento area and East Bay interests as a major achievement in regional cooperation. However, in a continuing period of competing needs, as periods of flood and drought alternate, balancing all demands becomes exceedingly difficult, and assuring adequate flows for fish and wildlife and for recreation requires constant vigilance by all those concerned with maintaining the quality of the American River and Parkway and its natural resources, uses and values.

River Water Quality

Public concern over water quality in a river flowing through a thickly populated region was heightened in the late 1990s by at least five sewage spills from the fast-growing city of Folsom into tributaries of the American River. They included a 700,000 gallon spill in January 2000 that resulted in the state fining the city $700,000 and requiring Folsom to develop a system to repair, replace and monitor its sewage collection system. The order set April, 2009 as the deadline for elimination of sewer outflows.

A Sacramento County Grand Jury investigation of the spills recommended that in view of the history of "aggressive growth" it said had been allowed by the city of Folsom, it should take no action to annex land south of Highway 50.

The City of Folsom reported in 2005 that it had met all state requirements for a national sewer discharge elimination permit, and had developed a plan to manage the inspection and preventative maintenance of the City's sewer system. Officials said this plan, initiated in 2002, has resulted in elimination of "reportable " spills exceeding 1,000 gallons and a 90 percent reduction in preventable spills of smaller volumes.

Chapter 7

Industry

This is the birth for us of Power, of Growth, of Greatness.
It is right that we should rejoice and celebrate it in this Grand
Electric Carnival, September 9, 1895.
— Sacramento Bee *editorial on first transmission of electrical power*

The American River was the focal point for much of Sacramento's early industry, which was either dependent upon water power generated by the American River, or was located on old mining lands adjacent to the river.

Sutter Period

The first major effort to harness this water power occurred in 1847 when John Sutter began construction of a grist or flour mill on the banks of the American River near Brighton. Sutter notes in his New Helvetia Diary on Nov. 30, 1847 that 34 men were employed in its construction.

> In 1847 I began to build a grist-mill on the American River at Brighton, about 4 miles above the Fort where I got a good fall of water by going back and making a dam and digging a race of four miles long.
> This mill was not completed when gold was discovered. I had everything ready, four pairs of mill stones, wheels, a large building erected, and it would have been all in working order in six months if the discovery of gold had been kept secret much longer … My grist-mill was never finished. Everything was stolen, even the stones.

In addition to his mill, Sutter also built a tannery near his original 1839 landing place on the banks of the American near present 28th and B Streets in Sacramento. Like his grist mill at Brighton, the tannery fell into disuse because there were no workers for hire after the discovery of gold. The tannery was a sizeable venture, using almost 100 processing vats to convert cowhide to leather. Sutter sold the property in 1848.

Another tannery in the vicinity of Sutter's Fort was owned by F. Rabel. It isn't known exactly when Rabel built his tannery, but it was operating in 1856. It was at the bend opposite Rabel's Tannery that the American River breached its north levee in January, 1862.

James Smith is credited with building the country's first operating, water-powered mill, a sawmill at Slate Bar near today's Negro Bar State Park on Lake Natoma in 1851. The following year he added a grist mill. He sold both properties to Edward Stockton in 1854. The floods of 1861-62 destroyed the mills along with Stockton's residence and gardens. Stockton rebuilt away from the river to avoid future floods. In 1865 the California Central Railroad ran a spur line to the new mills, but the mills burned in 1867 and were never rebuilt.

In 1854, S. L. Hunt erected the American River Sawmill. The mill was steam-powered, but the logs were supplied in great rafts that were floated to the mill on the American River. The mill was located on Water Street at the confluence of the American and Sacramento Rivers. By 1859, however, mining debris from the mountains had so filled the American River that log rafting became impossible during periods of low water. The machinery was moved to the Yolo County side of the Sacramento River just above Washington in 1859.

The presence of extensive granite and cobblestone deposits in the Folsom area prompted several efforts of commercial exploitation. The "*Thompson and West History of Sacramento County*" (1880) credits the infamous Colonel Russ (Ch. 2 — Ashland) with beginning the granite quarrying business in Sacramento County. Russ organized his company at Big Gulch (later Ashland), across the American River from Negro Bar in 1856 or 1857, using capital provided by San Francisco backers. It is more likely, however, that Griffith Griffiths was the first to quarry granite in the county at Slate Bar in 1856.

Natoma Company — Water And Power

Near Folsom Prison, Natoma Water and Mining Company owned a quarry that produced the granite used to build the first story of the present State Capitol and the prison.

The granite works provided lucrative freight. Carloads of granite destined for Sacramento and San Francisco and the government works at Fort Point in San Francisco crowded the Sacramento Front Street depot.

Granite traffic grew steadily and on Oct. 20, 1856 a record load of seven car loads of granite, approximately 70 tons, was hauled to Sacramento. The Folsom granite quarries could be counted on as a virtually unending source of profit to the Sacramento Valley Railroad (SVRR).

When viewing rock deposits in 1854, a reporter announced, "There is granite enough to supply the demand on the Pacific for the next thousand years."

Texas Hill downstream was a rich source of cobblestones which were used extensively in levee building and road paving:

For a number of years the trade in cobblestones, which were gathered along the American River, was very large. This district (Granite Township) supplied the great bulk of paving stones for San Francisco.

At Texas Hill the firm of Everett & Pardessus carried on the business from 1859 to 1860, when Everett retired, the price of cobbles having fallen to seventy-five cents a ton.

In 1863, the cobble pits at Texas Hill became the property of the Sacramento Valley Railroad Company which ... laid a branch track leading directly to the pits, thereby greatly facilitating the shipment of the rock.

Millions of tons of cobbles have been shipped from Folsom and vicinity, much the greater part of which has gone to San Francisco (*Thompson and West*)

Horatio Gates Livermore & Sons

Perhaps the most prominent industrialists identified with the American River in the latter part of the 19th century and early 20th were Horatio Gates Livermore and his sons Horatio Putnam Livermore and Charles Edward Livermore. The elder Livermore came to California from his native Livermore, Maine in 1850 and began mining on the American River near Georgetown. He quickly recognized the potential power of the American ... "to work our dirt ... or to run a saw mill or any other kinds of work requiring power."

In his letters to his family waiting in the East, Livermore provided insights into the miner's life in the early days of the gold rush. Of particular interest is his account of the north fork of the American River during the flood of 1852:

> … we had got everything complete, nearly, about the middle of Feb. & in a few days more would have been taking out gold, when the weather changed and storms continued for 3 weeks. You doubtless have heard the effects at Sacramento & other places. I know when you see in the papers that the American River was higher than in the freshet of '49 you will at once despair of my (water wheel) frame, but to the astonishment of all there it stood & there it stands 'calm as a summer morning.'
>
> We had completed the wheel, got it well in place, our pumps all complete for putting up, then the storm commenced. At first slowly snow on the mountains, rain below. In 5 or 6 days the weather became warm throughout the country and with the warm rain came down the melted snows. The river of course rose.
>
> We had our wheel high out of the water, higher than the first freshet. We put it together at that height to be out of danger till we get our ropes fixed to the windlass, when we can handle it at our pleasure. But the ropes we sent to the city for were not here yet. But up it rose.
>
> Presently the wheel began to spin around and dip deeper and deeper into the water. How it did run. The water, higher and higher, came up to the shaft. Over the shaft, then the wheel disappeared & a perfect half-moon of foam seemed to cover it up. The water still rose and came nearly to our floor. This I had put at 2 feet higher than the flood of '49. But the frame stood. The river had been rising for several days — but this was the evening of the highest rise. I saw it approach the floor with some apprehension.
>
> I went out onto the frame to see the river from it. I must say partly to show people that I was not afraid of the stability of my own handiwork. I had often looked down with almost a giddy feeling.
>
> Now up to my very feet … the whole void I had so often looked down upon was filled up with a raging mass of waters. I looked up the river. The whole chasm between the mountains was filled up, and it seemed as if a vast avalanche of liquid mud was rolling down towards me. The whole current was black, covered with drift. Trees 100 feet long & and all sorts of lesser trees on its surface, but the frame stood…

The year of 1856 was filled with events that combined to convince Livermore to settle in Folsom. A disastrous fire at Georgetown destroyed most of the buildings he owned. And when the Sacramento Valley Railroad was completed to Folsom, it seemed to Livermore that Folsom, rather than Georgetown, would lie on the route of the future transcontinental railroad. It was also in 1856 that his son, Horatio Putnam Livermore, arrived in California. Young Horatio described his father's interest in a letter home:

> His landed property at Folsom consists of some 350 lots, something more than fifty acres or about one-fifth of the town as laid out. For this he paid about $2,000, one hundred in cash and the remainder is now mortgaged on the lands.

The elder Livermore's evaluation of his prospects at Folsom are continued in a letter written in November, 1856 to his wife:

> I feel sure that my business at Folsom and at my place on the river above (a sawmill on the north fork of the American) will fully justify me in undertaking the expense of your house-keeping at the city (San Francisco) till I build at Folsom.

Part of the "business at Folsom" was Livermore's interest in the Natoma Water Company organized by Judge Catlin and others in 1851. By 1862, the Livermore family had gained control of Natoma Water and Mining and by 1866 were planning to dam the American River at Folsom as a pivotal step in Livermore's long-range plan to transform Folsom into a manufacturing center by harnessing the American River.

Central to the plan was a dam of granite and concrete at Folsom. It would provide a "still pond" to hold logs floated down from Livermore's logging operation on the Georgetown Divide. From the dam a 40-foot canal would lead downstream for a mile and a half, creating an 80-foot fall of water. This fall would generate the power to supply the envisioned factories at Folsom.

The dam and canal would be key elements in a lumber and manufacturing complex. Among the industries to be powered from the project were cotton and woolen mills, a paper-making plant and a carpet mill.

In addition to generating power, the company planned a massive project below Folsom, encompassing both sides of the American and extending to the Sacramento River. Storage reservoirs were to be constructed at Orange Vale and Roseville. Public reception of the proposal was not enthusiastic, so the plan was modified to include only land controlled by Natoma Water and Mining.

A key element to this project was the transfer of land to complete the dam and canal. Company and state officials disagreed over the rate of reimbursement to be given to the company, and this dispute delayed company plans. To clear up corporate complications, Livermore and his sons in 1881 formed the Folsom Water Power Company and assumed all rights and properties of Natoma Water and Mining that pertained to water power.

> A proposed franchise to establish a lumber market at the dam of the Folsom Water Company near Folsom was put before the (Sacramento) County Board of Supervisors. This company wanted to build a saw mill and a sash, door and blind factory. They also wanted to establish a boom to catch and hold sawlogs for anyone who wanted to float them down the American.
>
> However, the river must be prepared before logs can successfully be floated down the river by blowing out rocks. It is claimed by this company's opposition that this lumber market might interfere with vested mining and water rights.
>
> However logs can be floated at a time when the water is too high for mining. Logs must be floated within a 30-day period each year. (*Sacramento Record Union*, 1899)

Construction of the dam at Stony Bar began in 1867. Natoma Water and Mining built the foundation of the dam and brought the initial height up to 30 feet. It was at this point that financing became a problem and the company entered negotiations with the State to exchange land for the prison site for convict labor.

As the years passed and work was delayed on the dam and canal project, the directors of Natoma Water and Mining became disenchanted, and it was agreed that Livermore and his son would buy out the company interest. Under this agreement, the work moved toward completion in 1888.

Logging began in June, 1890 and a year later the first logs reached Folsom Dam. This first drive clearly showed that the bed of the American River needed extensive work to clear obstacles and allow the logs to float freely down the river. Another difficulty was that after the logs entered the still pond behind Folsom Dam they covered the surface, and many were washed over the top by flood waters and were lost. Still another difficulty was the fact that for logs to reach the sawmill at Folsom, they had to be floated from the dam via the State Prison canal. Prison officials were reluctant to adjust the headgates of the canal for fear that the logs might interfere with prison power plant operations.

Difficulties continued over the next few years. To prevent logs from floating over Folsom Dam, a log boom was built in the still pond behind the dam. This barricade broke, and the winter drive of logs for 1892-93 had to be called off. The following year the drive, consisting of three million feet of logs, was stranded at Salmon Falls because of low water and couldn't reach Folsom that year. During the winter of 1894-95, high water held long enough to float logs stranded at Salmon Falls down the river, and an additional four million feet of logs were started down from the Georgetown Divide. The company was encouraged to begin building its sawmill in 1895, and completed it in December 1896. The mill operated on electric power generated at Folsom and could cut 75,000 board feet of lumber per day.

No sooner had the company completed the sawmill than a disagreement between company and prison officials broke out. It was feared that logs in the prison canal would make prisoner escape a simple matter. With no means of supplying the mill with logs, it shut down in March, 1897 and remained idle through the following year.

The season of 1898-99 was the last one in which the American River Land and Lumber Company operated. Twenty million feet of logs were in readiness for the run to Folsom. In March 1899, the rains came, the water rose, and the drive down the river began. The water behind Folsom Dam was covered with logs, creating too great a strain in the log boom. When the log boom broke, almost three million feet of logs were swept over the dam and scattered from Folsom to Rio Vista in the Delta. This last blow was too much and the company assets were attached by creditors and sold. In later years an early logger recalled:

> They sent for the finest river drivers they could find. They sent to Canada for most of them, they were fine men, all over six feet and tough. They were hard working, hard drinking men but this river just couldn't be drove.
> They used tons and tons of powder trying to make a channel. It was just about impossible to move out a key log when there was a jam like they do back home. The logs were just too heavy. I used to write home about the condition of the river and the size of the logs, big six and seven-foot sticks, but they wouldn't believe me.

The elder Livermore never lived to see his plans realized. He died in Oakland on Jan. 13, 1892. The dam was completed almost one year later, and water was turned into the canal in January, 1893.

Electric Power

Although Folsom never became the industrial center that Livermore envisioned, it did figure prominently in the development of a basic ingredient of industry — electric power.

Horatio Putnam Livermore

Great strides had taken place in power engineering during the 27 years which intervened between start and completion of the dam. During those years young Horatio Putnam Livermore assumed more and more responsibility for leading his father's enterprises. Electricity replaced water as industry's power source, and Horatio Putnam Livermore had the foresight to take advantage of this system in Sacramento and formed the Sacramento Electric Power and Light Company in 1892 to supply the power.

Again financing was a problem. The depression of the 1890s severely curtailed capital available for investment. At this point, Livermore became associated with another enterprising Sacramento businessman, Albert Gallatin. Gallatin began his career in Sacramento as a clerk at the Huntington-Hopkins hardware company and rose to become president and general manager of this "Big Four" railroad venture. Gallatin completed a series of financial maneuvers and provided the needed capital for the new power company.

By July, 1895 all generating transmission equipment was ready for testing, and on July 10 a test at Folsom was satisfactorily completed. A second test the next afternoon, however, failed because of crossed wires near Brighton. At 4 a.m., July 13, a 100-gun salute fired on the banks of China Slough announced the final success of the project. By October the powerhouse was in full operation, capable of generating 3,000 kilowatts of power.

Sacramento staged an elaborate "Electric Carnival" to celebrate the world's first long-distance transmission of electrical power from the source at Folsom to Sacramento. By today's standards, the 22 miles from Folsom to Sacramento is hardly "long distance," but in 1895 it represented an almost miraculous achievement. So little was known about electricity that it was feared it might lose power going around corners, so builders kept the lines as straight as possible. The brick substation at 6th and H streets where the power entered Sacramento is still in use. .

The idea for an Electric Carnival to formally celebrate the achievement originated with the *Sacramento Bee*. Citizens responded to the idea enthusiastically, and on Admission Day, Sept. 9, 1895, Sacramento was ready. A night parade of illuminated floats passed under elaborately lighted arches over the streets, and the Capitol glowed in incandescent glory which could be seen 50 miles away. A *Bee* editorial stated:

> This is the birth for us of Power, of Growth, of Greatness. It is right that we should rejoice and celebrate it in this Grand Electric Carnival, September 9, 1895.

Folsom Power House (1895-1952) transmitted the new AC current to Sacramento over the first long-distance power line (22 miles) in the world. The power house is now a unit of the State Park System.

The State Capitol was lit up for the 1895 Electric Carnival, in celebration of the World's first long-distance transmission of electric power.

The powerhouse at Folsom is still standing, a monument to Livermore's foresight and perseverance. From its beginning in 1894 the powerhouse was in continuous operation until 1952, using much of the original equipment. In 1952, the Pacific Gas and Electric Co. presented the building to the State of California and it was dedicated as part of the State Park System. It is both a National and State Historical Landmark. Guided tours are provided by the Friends of Folsom Power House, a volunteer association formed to assist State Parks in interpretive programs.

Aerospace

U.S. involvement in World War I had a significant and lasting impact on industrial development along the American River corridor. With an $18 million contract to build airplanes, the Liberty Iron Works in North Sacramento was committed to deliver airplane No. 1 in less than five weeks and the first 30 planes due by Nov. 1, 1917. After this initial 30, Liberty Iron was to produce 150 planes each month. The airplane being built in Sacramento was the famous Curtiss JN-4 or "Jenny." A whole generation of Americans learned to fly in Jennies and, in addition to U.S. and Canadian pilots, flying schools in Great Britain and France used them as trainers. After the war, thousands were sold to civilians and the plane had a second career as a barnstorming plane, thrilling spectators at traveling aerial shows throughout the United States.

The Sacramento Chamber of Commerce campaigned to have an aviator training school located in the county, and in February 1918 completed a lease agreement with the War Department for 789 acres near Mills, now Rancho Cordova, as a site for the flying

The famous "Jenny" of World War I was manufactured at the hurriedly converted Liberty Iron Works in Sacramento.

school. The land belonged to the Natomas Company which offered to lease the land at $1 per year for five years.

The training school was originally called Mills Station Aviation School, but in May 1918 the name was changed to honor Second Lieutenant Carl Spenser Mather, who had been killed in a training flight collision in Texas earlier that year. Aviation training began at Mather Field on June 12, 1918 when four aviators made the first official flight, piloting Curtiss "Jennies" built at the Liberty Iron Works.

After WWII, Mather AFB trained aerial navigators for the U.S. military and allies and, until 1989, U.S. B-52s were based there. As world tensions eased, Mather was decommissioned as an active air base in 1993. Most of the base was declared surplus and transferred or leased, mainly to Sacramento County. Mather's air field was reopened as an air cargo field. Other occupants are a business park, single family and transitional housing, regional park, golf course, veterans hospital, and sports complex.

Aerojet General

With the advent of America's space age, Natomas properties became host of another industrial development, Aerojet General. The corporation announced in December, 1950 that it would build a $6 million rocket factory at Nimbus on land purchased from the Natomas Company. More than 90 percent of company production involved Air Force projects.

By 1957 Aerojet had grown to include 20,000 acres and had expended more that $60 million in the construction of rocket production facilities. Ten years later, Aerojet was the largest rocket production plant in the western hemisphere. In the 1970s, as need diminished for large scale rocket production, the Rancho Cordova-headquartered subsidiary of GenCorp Co. began diversifying into new areas, such as pharmaceutical chemicals.

By 2005, Aerojet was continuing to deal with a water quality issue dating back to 1979. It was discovered then that rocket fuel compounds from the early days of the aerospace boom had seeped from holding ponds into the soil and groundwater under the Rancho Cordova plant. The company launched a major clean-up effort at that time, treating groundwater and reinjecting it into the aquifer. However, around 1997, emerging issues with previously undetected levels of the contaminants perchlorate and NDMA required Aerojet to recapture and retreat the previously treated water a second time. By this time, the reinjected groundwater had migrated several hundreds of feet deep under portions of Rancho Cordova and partially under Carmichael across the river in 2004.

This discovery required closure of a number of Rancho Cordova drinking water wells. Aerojet provided replacement water and financial compensation for affected water purveyors in Rancho Cordova while crafting a groundwater remedy. Aerojet immediately crafted a remediation plan for capturing and treating contaminated groundwater and began implementation of the remedy in Rancho Cordova and Carmichael. The remedy consists of a series of groundwater extraction wells designed to prevent further migration of the plume, allowing for the removal and treatment of the contaminants. Treated water is then released to public waterways, allowing for reuse.

Another aerospace related industry located on Natomas land was the McDonnell-Douglas Company's Sacramento Test Center. By 1964 McDonnell-Douglas had control of 4,000 acres and was heavily involved in testing and checking Saturn rocket stages used in NASA's Apollo lunar spacecraft project.

Like Aerojet, McDonnell-Douglas cut back on its activities at the Test Center in the 1970s, and the land has since converted into an industrial park.

Aerojet General inaugurated Sacramento's space age in the 1950s by building a rocket plant on land south of Folsom purchased from the Natomas Company. By 1967, it was the largest rocket production plant in the Western Hemisphere.

SACRAMENTO VALLEY MONTHLY

CALIFORNIA

DECEMBER, 1911

24c Per Year

Vol. 1. No. 7

A MAGAZINE DEVOTED TO PROGRESS IN CALIFORNIA

Official Publication of the Sacramento Valley Development Association---A Public Organization

*Oranges were
an important crop in
the Orangevale, Citrus Heights,
and Fair Oaks areas at the turn of the century.*

Chapter 8

Agriculture
Sutter Period

After the (Mexican-American) war things prospered for me. I found a good market for my products among the newcomers and the people in the Bay district. Agriculture increased until I had several hundred men working in the harvest fields, and to feed them I had to kill four or sometimes five oxen daily. I could raise 40,000 bushels of wheat without trouble. There were thirty plows running with fresh oxen each morning. I had at that time twelve thousand head of cattle, two thousand horses and mules, between ten and fifteen thousand sheep, and a thousand hogs. My best days were just before the discovery of gold."
— *From "Sutter's Own Story," By Erwin Gudde, 1936.*

John Sutter was first to practice European-style agriculture in the American River area. In September, 1841, he outlined some of his plans to a visiting Frenchman, Deflot De Mofras. The Frenchman later wrote that Sutter expected to export grain, vegetables, butter and cheese. He also intended to cultivate rice, cotton, indigo, grapes, olives and other fruit on a large scale. Unfortunately, fate had other plans.

John Bidwell, later one of California's most distinguished citizens, arrived in the Sacramento Valley in late 1841, and for a time was employed by Sutter. In his memoirs, Bidwell described one of Sutter's wheat harvests:

> Imagine three or four hundred ... Indians in a grain field, armed, some with sickles, some with butcher knives, some with pieces of hoop iron roughly fashioned like sickles, but many having only their hands with which to gather by small handfuls the dry and brittle grain; and as their hands would soon become sore, they resorted to dry willow sticks, which were split to afford a sharper edge with which to sever the straw.
> But the wildest part was the thrashing. The harvest of weeks sometimes of a month, was piled up in the straw in the form of a huge mound in the middle of a high, strong, round corral; then three or four hundred wild horses were turned in to thrash it, the Indians whooping to make them run faster.
> Suddenly they would dash in before the band at full speed, when the motion became reversed, with the effect of plowing up the trampled straw to the very bottom.
> In an hour the grain would be thoroughly thrashed and the dry straw bro-

ken almost to chaff. In this manner I have seen two thousand bushels of wheat thrashed in a single hour.

Next came the winnowing, which would often take another month. It could only be done when the wind was blowing, by throwing high into the air shovelfuls of grain, straw and chaff, the lighter material being wafted to one side, while the grain, comparatively clean, would descend and form a heap by itself.

In that manner all the grain in California was cleaned. At that day no such thing as a fanning mill had ever been brought to the coast.

Gold Rush And After

Smith's Gardens

But the best known early agricultural beneficiary of Lower American water was A.P. Smith, founder of the Pomological Gardens and Nursery on the south bank of the river on the eastern outskirts of Sacramento. Smith purchased more than 50 acres from Sutter in December, 1849 and began cultivating seeds and nursery stock for sale to valley growers. By 1858 Smith had expanded his nursery to 90 acres:

> Two and one-half miles from Sacramento City, on the same side of the American River, are the Pomological Gardens and Nursery of A. P. Smith, who devotes his time and attention to the cultivation of fruits, flowers, nursery, and vegetable seeds.
>
> His place contains ninety acres, twenty of which are devoted exclusively to the growing of vegetable seeds for the trade, about six to buildings and pleasure-grounds and the remainder to orchard, vineyard and nursery.
>
> The orchard consists of peach-trees, one thousand five hundred; pear, (standard) ninety-five, and dwarf eight thousand and sixty-eight; plum, two hundred and forty; apricot, two hundred and one; cherry, three hundred and sixty-nine; apple, two hundred and sixty; nectarine, one hundred and forty; grapes, (California) one thousand five hundred; currants and gooseberries, two hundred; strawberries, four acres; raspberries, one acre.

Hauling a load of hops, once one of Sacramento area's major crops.

Mr. S. is careful to cultivate only such varieties as are best adapted to this climate.

Flower-Garden and Green-House — In this department Mr. Smith has also been entirely successful. Though justice to so fine a place and to such enterprise would seem to demand an extended enumeration of the plants and shrubs raised by Mr. S., yet our want of space forbids. In the collection are to be found more than fifteen thousand roses, embracing all the new and choicest varieties, as well as the old favorites.

There are also, two thousand camellias, of vigorous growth, and in fine healthy condition.

Vegetable-Seed Department — To this department Mr. Smith turned especial attention at an early day, and has pursued it, till now he devotes to it twenty acres of ground, and the time of several laborers and from it reaps a merited reward. His crop of seeds for the past four years has reached from three to four thousand pounds per annum.

In the matter of irrigation, Mr. Smith ... has provided himself with a ten-horsepower steam engine, attached to a Worthington pump, and placed the same in proximity to the (American) river. With this apparatus he elevates water to a tank fourteen feet above the common level of his grounds, at the rate of three hundred and fifty thousand gallons in twelve hours. From this tank (containing about ten thousand gallons) the water is conducted underground, in earthen pipes, made in Sacramento, to all parts of the place.

To perform the labor necessary to the thorough cultivation of this great stock, and variety of products, requires an average of about thirty men the entire year. (California Agriculture Society Transactions, 1859.)

Brighton

Beyond Smith's gardens to the east, the fertile land along the river supported a variety of agricultural ventures. Agricultural activity in the vicinity of what is now the CSUS campus was responsible in part for the establishment and growth of the town of Brighton.

Sutter himself had planned to build a grist mill in this area in 1847, but the gold strike at Coloma lured his workers away and the mill was never finished. In August, 1850 Brighton achieved the grim distinction of being the place where Sacramento's. Sheriff McKinney was shot to death as a result of Sacramento's "Squatter's Riot." The town was abandoned in 1852 because of land title difficulties, although a surviving hotel, the "Five Mile House" was used as a Pony Express remount station in 1860-61.

The Brighton area contained the state's most extensive hop fields. Cultivation of hops was economically important for its use in brewing and was begun at a rather early date:

I (Daniel Flint) claim to be the first man on the coast that discovered that hops would bear the first year they were planted.

After planting my hop roots in the winter of 1857-58 in Sacramento, I was told by one of my neighbors not to pole them, as they would surely go to vines, without hops, everything being of such a rank growth in this rich soil.

The earliest importation of hop roots, to the best of my knowledge, was in 1855-56 by Wilson Flint, from Vermont, and propagated in Alameda until moved to Sacramento in the winter of 1857-58.

I claim to have built the first hop kiln and first hop press on this coast, and to engage in it as a commercial business.

The horsepower press that is used mostly on this coast is my invention, and is capable of putting out from forty to sixty bales per day of two hundred pounds each.

Good hop land can be bought from $100 to $400 per acre depending upon quality and location. Suitable hop land can be leased for a term of years for from $20 to $30 per acre.

There is no county in the State or on the coast that has such facilities for the transportation of hops, wood, coal, poles, or help for picking as Sacramento.

At the present time the future conundrum seems to be, where shall we procure our help to pick our vast hop yards? If there is any place where they can be secured it is at Sacramento. This seems to be the stopping place, or half-way house for transient help from mines, fields, and roads.

Our harvest time is free from rain, wind, or frost, which cause such great loss in other locations. The pickers can camp in the open field, needing no shelter, without serious inconvenience.

Only one variety (of hop), the large American, is cultivated to any extent on this coast. Planting takes place in January or February. Tying vines to poles begins from May 1st to 10th. Picking begins about August 20th and continues from four to six weeks. The price is from 80 cents to $1 per hundred, of green hops.

Pickers can make from $1 to $2.50 per day, according to expertness and condition of hops. The pickers range in nationality in the order named: Chinese, Indians, Whites, and Japanese.

There is hop land enough on this coast to supply the world. Our growers are using the most modern appliances in culture, harvesting, and curing, such as draft kiln, heaters, pipe and horse-power press. (California State Agricultural Society Transactions, 1891)

The Brighton area was also noted for its orchards and vineyards, and 1870 saw the introduction of sugar-beet farming with a large factory to process the beets. The factory, owned by the Sacramento Valley Sugar Beet Company, was located at the intersection of J Street and the American River levee. The plant could produce up to 100 tons of sugar daily. The main building was surrounded by a company-owned lodging and boarding house, storehouse, cooper shop, tool house and stables.

The company farmed 1,400 acres, including 500 acres rented near Davis. The land produced about one ton of beets per acre. At the height of the season 500 men were employed in processing the sugar-beets. This included 300 Chinese field hands.

In 1873 the company adopted a novel approach in combating an attack of army-worms. Five-hundred turkeys that were released:

> … soon turned the evil into good. In a few days they gobbled up the army, and converted it into rich and profitable meat. Hereafter a turkey ranch will form a necessary supplement to the sugary and its profits will excel those of the fatted cattle that feed upon the offal at the mill. (*Pacific Rural Press*)

Near the sugar factory the company built the Capital Distillery, which manufactured "wines of first, second, and third quality from molasses of the beets." A second distillery — not connected with the beet company — also operated in the Brighton area beginning in 1875, producing 10,000 gallons of brandy annually from locally-grown grapes.

Wheat production in the Brighton area was a profitable endeavor:

> Good Yield — One hundred and twenty acres of wheat land belonging to John B. Taylor in the upper end of Brighton Township, produced thirty bushels to the acre this season (1873). The farmers in upper Brighton are good farmers. They generally fallow their land, which produces good crops, and as a consequence they are gradually growing rich. (*Pacific Rural Press*)

Whether or not Brighton farmers were "becoming rich," they were aware that to maintain a reasonable return on their farm investment, they needed to be organized politically, the *Rural Press* proclaimed:

> ... (farmers) have learned that in other industrial pursuits, as also in the business and professional world, everybody organized but the farmers, and that they would not soon become the helpless and impoverished victims of combinations they must organize and fraternize.

As a result of such agitation, Brighton farmers became involved in the Farmer's Movement and organized the American River Grange in 1873, W. S. Manlove, Master. Brighton's grange was the 12th grange organized in California.

Folsom

The present-day Bradshaw Road marks the division line between Sutter and Leidesdorff grants. In the agricultural sense, this boundary is artificial, because the character of the land and its productivity are essentially the same. There was a difference in how the land was farmed, however, and as one progressed eastward from Sutter's grant the emphasis shifted from hops to grapes.

Within the limits of the Leidesdorff grant, farmers were faced with uncertain titles to the land until the matter was settled in the courts. William Leidesdorff, the original grantee, died in 1848 and there was a disagreement between his heirs and the purchaser of the land, Joseph L. Folsom. Leidesdorff's mother, who lived in the Danish West Indies, felt that Folsom had misrepresented the value of the land and on that basis sought to have her agreement to sell to Folsom set aside.

Folsom's right to the land was established by the California Land Grant Commission in 1855. Folsom himself died in 1856 and "squatters" took this as a signal to occupy the land as public domain. To further complicate matters, the original boundaries of the grant had been set in a most informal manner, consisting of Sutter and Leidesdorff riding on horseback to the "lomeria" or foothills which they agreed would be the eastern boundary of the Leidesdorff property.

The problem was officially settled in late 1864 when President Lincoln affixed his signature to the patent and ended the bitter, sometimes violent, disagreement on the boundary question. Perhaps the most painful "loser" in this struggle was one William Tenant whose nose was bitten off in an argument over property ownership.

As finally adjudicated, the northern boundary was declared to be the American River, extending from Bradshaw Road eastward to within ¼ mile of the junction of the North and South Forks of the American above Folsom. The patent, based on A. P. Jones' survey of 1857, established the western boundary at an oak tree on the south bank of the American, on the edge of A. D. Patterson's property. The town of Folsom was included in the area grant. A.P. Catlin, a man prominent in the formation of the original Natoma Company, was the attorney who successfully argued the case before the U. S. Supreme Court.

Newell Kane, a pioneer farmer, described the area in 1853: "The land was covered with brush and trees, mostly white oak, and wild animals were plentiful, the California lion and wild cattle causing at times great fear among the settlers."

Many of those who took up farming along the American River did so after returning to Sacramento from the mines. Joseph Routier, however, came specifically "for the purpose of superintending the planting of a large vineyard and orchard for Captain Folsom."

In 1853 Routier moved into the old Leidesdorff adobe and began his task. At the request of Folsom heirs, he carried on with the project even after Folsom's death in 1856.

Routier set a precedent in cultivating grapes rather than wheat. Because of his success, the American River region was "among the first in California to establish large-scale farming in orchards and vineyards".

By 1863 Routier was able to purchase the acreage he worked from Folsom heirs. He grew prunes, walnuts, apricots, peaches, almonds and oranges. He is credited with introducing the Flame Tokay grape for which the region became noted. Routier produced his own wine, and in 1876 built a fruit drying and canning plant on his ranch which processed 40,000 cans of fruit annually. He was so successful as a fruit grower that the railroad scheduled a loading stop at his ranch and named it in his honor.

Natoma

In many cases throughout the mining country, the water supply systems that were originally constructed to supply the mines later became valuable in the irrigation of agricultural lands. Such was the case with the Natoma Water Company, organized by a group headed by A. P. Catlin. The company's purpose was to bring water into the Folsom area for placer-mining the land, which was otherwise of relatively little value. Catlin's group built a diversion dam at Salmon Falls on the south fork of the American River, and a canal to bring water to the "dry diggings." In 1852 the company filed notice in Placerville of its intent to appropriate water "by means of Natoma Canal." These water rights are still owned by the present Natomas Company and are the oldest rights of their type recognized in California.

In 1853 Natoma Water Company reorganized as the Natoma Water and Mining Company, a joint stock venture. Horatio Gates Livermore and his sons gained control of the company in 1862. The eldest Livermore foresaw a more extensive use of the water from the American River than merely mining, and the company became involved in a comprehensive development of the power and irrigation potential of the dam and canal system. Company projects included construction of the original Folsom dam and of the Folsom Prison; granite-quarrying; production of paving cobbles, crushed rock and aggregate; placer and dredge mining; development of both water and hydro-electric power; and extensive agricultural development and land reclamation.

Natoma Water and Mining Company became actively engaged in agriculture shortly after Horatio Gates Livermore took control. As its mining claims were worked out, it planted the land in grape vines and orchards. Some vines were planted in the 1860s, though the most extensive plantings occurred during 1883-84. At that time the Natoma vineyards covered some 2,000 acres and were the largest in the world. In time they would be surpassed in size only by those at Vina, Tehama County, owned by Leland Stanford. In addition to the vineyards, the Natoma Company built and operated a winery at Nimbus. In 1888 company officials decided to re-charter as Natoma Vineyard Company to reflect their major business.

The company also owned orchards of pears, peaches, prunes, and olives. Across the railroad tracks from the company cottages at Natoma, a group of Indian commercial vegetable farmers grew crops on land leased from Natoma Vineyard. Some idea of the range of company activities during the 1870s can be gained from the following item which appeared in the *Pacific Rural Press* in 1873:

Sacramento — The Natoma Water & Mining Company are running several gang plows on the land at Alder Creek and are also doing considerable work at the granite quarries, and on the canal designed for manufacturing purposes. The railroad leading from Folsom to the quarries has been placed in fine running order. Cobbles are again in active demand in San Francisco, where wood pavements have fallen into disrepute.

The portion of Sutter's grant north of the river included the present Reclamation District 1000. This "American Basin" was a swamp-and-overflowed area in Sutter's time and remained so until reclaimed by Natomas Consolidated of California, successor to the Natoma Water and Mining and Natoma Vineyard companies. Natomas Consolidated began draining the land and constructing levees and ditches in 1911, and soon the rich river bottom lands were producing corn, tomatoes, row-crops and beans.

Boston

There was an early attempt to establish a city on the north bank of the river near the mouth, but it never progressed beyond "paper city" status. It was described by E. Gould Buffum in 1850 as follows:

> The City of Boston is located on the north bank of the American River, at its junction with the Sacramento River about one hundred yards above the old embarcadero, the site on which the city of Sacramento now stands.
>
> It extends upon the banks of both rivers for several miles and is destined to become a great and flourishing city. The banks of the Sacramento at that point are not subject to overflow, being more than twelve feet in many places above the high-water mark.
>
> The town is situated on a broad and well-watered plain covered with many groves of magnificent oaks, and the largest class of steamers and all vessels navigating the Sacramento River can lie and discharge directly at its banks.
>
> The direct and most-traveled road proceeds from this point to the rich placers of Yuba, Feather, Middle and South Forks of American Rivers.
>
> The soil is of the richest description, the surrounding scenery highly picturesque, and the plains in the immediate vicinity are covered with wild game of every variety which California affords.

Natomas farm stock harnessed for work.

The present owner is Hiram Grimes. Lots are selling rapidly at from $200 to
$1000 each and before many months the city of Boston on the golden banks of the
Rio Sacramento will rival its New England namesake in business and importance.

The *Union* reported that the above read like fiction to many people. In 1849-50, the
site was covered with long rows of white tents, but was uninhabitable for several months
of the year, being overflowed land.

Rancho del Paso

Fronting the north bank of the American River and adjoining Sutter's grant to the
west was the Rancho del Paso grant. The boundary between the grants corresponds to
present-day Northgate Boulevard. The Rancho del Paso grant contained more than 44,000
acres and extended eastward along the American to the Fair Oaks-Manzanita Avenue line
in Carmichael. The name was taken from a ford across the river near the H Street Bridge
which was known as "el paso de los Americanos" (the pass of the Americans).

Mexican Governor Manuel Micheltorena awarded the grant to Eliab Grimes in 1844.
Grimes was a merchant doing business in Honolulu when he visited California in 1838.
He was impressed with the land and made another visit in 1842 at which time he selected
the site of his grant, next to Sutter's. Grimes took up permanent residence in San
Francisco and engaged the Scotsman, John Sinclair, to act as his agent and look after his
American River property. Sinclair moved to the Rancho in 1842 and was a frequent visitor
and friend of Sutter. Sinclair probably became acquainted with Grimes in Honolulu,
where Sinclair edited a newspaper.

Edwin Bryant mentions Sinclair and the Rancho during a visit to Sacramento in
September 1846:

> We reached the residence of John Sinclair, Esq. on the Rio de los
> Americanos about two miles east of Sutter's Fort. The composition of the soil
> appears to be such as to render it highly productive, with proper cultivation, of
> the small grain.
> The ground is trodden upon by immense herds of cattle and horses which
> grazed here early in the spring, when it was wet and apparently mirey ... We
> passed through large evergreen oak groves, some of them miles in width.
> Game is very abundant. We frequently saw deer feeding quietly one or two
> hundred yards from us, and large flocks of antelope.

Historian Hubert Howe Bancroft said Grimes kept a case of extra fine liquor at his
home in San Francisco, and the only way to get the old man to open a bottle of this
choice stock was to tell a story that aroused his interest. As can be imagined, Grimes was
kept much amused by the younger merchants of the city. It is said that during the gold
rush up to Sacramento in 1849 someone asked if there was anyone left in San Francisco.
"Nobody but Grimes," was the reply. The story is, sadly, apocryphal for "old Grimes" died
in October, 1848 at the age of 69.

In 1849 after Grimes' death his nephew and partner, Hiram Grimes, sold the Rancho
to Samuel Norris. Norris was a native of Denmark; his real name was Gotthild Willhelm
Becher Christensen. Just why he assumed the name Samuel Norris is not clear. However,
there are no suspicious events in his record to indicate that he was a fugitive like many
others who used an alias in California.

Norris was a cantankerous sort, and therefore a frequent visitor to the courtroom as
a litigant. Before the year 1849 was out, he was involved in a court battle over the terms of

a lease he had given to William Muldrow to raise crops and cattle on the Rancho. The transcript of the case places a hog farm, dairy cows, and wheat fields along the American River on Norris' property during 1849-50. The dispute between Norris and Muldrow eventually went all the way to the state Supreme Court. Testimony before the court reveals that crops worth $9,000 were produced on the 20-acre plot.

All claims to Mexican grants had to be confirmed by a special federal land commission which sat in San Francisco. As a claimant of Rancho del Paso, Norris was represented by the law partners James B. Haggin and Lloyd Tevis. Norris' claim was recognized as valid in 1857. In 1862 Haggin and Tevis, who held a $65,000 mortgage on the Rancho, secured title from Norris for an additional $5,000.

In 1884 Norris brought suit to have the title returned to him. He claimed that during the years between 1857 and 1883 he was not in his "right mind" as the result of a blow on the head. His suit was not successful.

Under Haggin's ownership the Rancho was initially used for pasture. Sheep were imported from Australia in the 1870s, and by 1884 there were 20,000 sheep, cattle and horses grazing on the uplands of the Rancho. The bottom-lands, some 8,000 acres, were planted in grain, hay and hops.

In 1881 Haggin began breeding thoroughbred horses on a large scale. Horse breeding was carried on at two main locations: Ben Ali station on the Southern Pacific Railroad route, and "The Bottom" on the river near the intersection of modern Watt Avenue and Arden Way. Twenty-four barns, some having as many as sixty-four stalls, were built to shelter Haggin's horses. Two full-sized race tracks provided training facilities.

In 1885 Haggin horses won more than $125,000 in purse money, the largest amount ever won by a single stable during a season at that time. Ben Ali, a Haggin entry, won the Kentucky Derby in 1886.

The stables of James Ben Ali Haggin at Rancho del Paso included some of the nation's most famous race horses. One of them, Ben Ali, won the Kentucky Derby in 1886.

Haggin held an annual auction sale of his stock in New York. In 1905 he decided that the breeding business was no longer profitable and shipped 524 horses to New York for a final sale. This shipment required 48 railroad cars to move the animals. Haggin's own estimate of the worth of these horses was in excess of $1.25 million. With the departure of horses, the Rancho was used to raise cattle.

Haggin wanted to sell his property, but insisted that the grant be purchased in one piece. From 1905 until 1909 no purchaser with sufficient capital was interested. In 1905 Haggin was asking $2 million; however, the reported sale price in 1909 was just $1.5 million.

North Sacramento

On May 10, 1909 the United States Farm Land Company, Minneapolis-St Paul, assumed ownership of the Rancho. A subsidiary, the Sacramento Valley Colonization Company, was incorporated in Phoenix, AZ to handle the task of subdivision and sale of the Rancho property. D. W. Johnston of Sacramento organized the North Sacramento Land Co. which purchased 4,400 acres from the subsidiary and began an extensive plan for developing the area. This property fronted on the American River beginning at the western boundary of the original grant, and extending eastward to the Southern Pacific Railroad Bridge. The property extended beyond Arcade Creek and included 825 acres purchased by the city for Del Paso Park.

A *Sunset Magazine* advertisement by the North Sacramento Land Company in its campaign to settle North Sacramento carried a picture of Arcade Creek wandering through a lovely pastoral scene, and boasted:

> No city ever possessed a more beautiful, alluring and attractive suburb than the city of Sacramento has in "North Sacramento." This beautiful tract of four thousand acres adjoining the city of Sacramento on the north is being subdivided into high-class suburban and villa homesites. Every condition surrounds this magnificent property to insure delightful suburban life.
>
> For transportation there are three distinct railway lines passing through it. In fifteen minutes time you are on gently rolling land, among tall and stately oaks. You can secure a homesite or a five-acre tract for from $250 to $500 per acre.
>
> The soil is especially adapted to most intensive cultivations. Water for domestic purposes will be supplied at a small monthly rental, and for irrigation purposes an abundance of semi-artesian water lies from ten to fifteen feet below the surface.

The North Sacramento Land Company was extremely successful in its campaign. However, the river lands to the east continued to be primarily agricultural. Hop fields, vegetable gardens and orchards were maintained in the rich "bottoms" as far east as the river bluffs near Folsom. Vegetables were grown along the river from its confluence with the Sacramento to three or four miles up stream, and on toward Folsom extended hop fields, alfalfa and orchards.

Chapter 9

Land Colonization

Conveniences here (Carmichael) embrace electric light and power, telephone,
daily mail, churches, schoolhouses and quick connections by mail to
Sacramento City. Vegetables and garden truck mature early. Fowls thrive and
the owner of a tract may be as independent as a king in his castle. Eternal
summer — no snow — no frost — no cyclones — no sunstrokes. We have
our rainy season in the winter which corresponds to the snow season
back East — this however, is not a drawback but a blessing.

— *Sunset magazine 'promotional article,' May 1911*

By the late 1800s "the West was Won" and a new wave of emigrants poured from the chilly East and Midwest to the land of orange groves and palm trees. Many were lured by railroads seeking settlers to grow crops for trains to haul and people to occupy the towns along the railroad routes.

Agricultural colonies, more or less utopian in nature, were the popular thing; perhaps people felt more secure starting out in a group enterprise. And Sacramento did its best to attract its share of the new gold rush, as the few remaining palm trees and orange groves in the lands along the river today attest.

Most colonies had a similar history; though the initial dream usually proved impossible, eventually a more solid economic base evolved. The original promoters would probably be astounded to discover how far beyond their wildest speculations their bare cropland had developed.

Sacramento was a land promoter's paradise. The area had fine soil and a good climate, and water was readily available. In the latter part of the nineteenth century several land colonies were formed for the purpose of subdividing the area near the American River.

San Juan Grant

The 20,000-acre San Juan Grant was the chosen site. By 1880 this grant had changed hands many times, mostly because the owners were unable to pay the taxes assessed, and it fell into the hands of a real estate firm, Cox & Clark of Sacramento, which used the land for cattle grazing. Then John T. Cardwell bought 4,000 acres in 1881 with the idea of clearing the land and selling the wood in Sacramento. By 1886, he had 40,000 cords of wood ready to be hauled by barge to the city. Then his project was besieged by transportation difficulties and he was forced to sell the southern half of his property in 1887.

Orange Vale

The purchaser of the land was the Orange Vale Colonization Company, a group of 30 Sacramento businessmen. T. B. Hall was president of the company, which included V. S. McClatchy, George M. Mott, P. C. Drescher and H. Weinstock. At the same time an old mining ditch had been bought by the American River Ditch Company, which had planted 10,000 orange trees during the spring of 1887. During the winter of 1888 the company lost its trees to the cold, and the ditch was sold to Cox and Clark, which renamed it the North Fork Ditch. The ditch was used to bring water to the Orange Vale colony.

Orange Vale Colony was a well-planned subdivision, "with avenues running east and west every quarter mile, and spaced at half-mile intervals in a north-south direction so that every ten-acre plot fronted on a street." Orange Vale did not specialize in the production of one type of crop. The colony was meant to be a "striking illustration" of self-sufficient small farming. J. W. Anderson, an experienced fruit farmer, was the pioneer superintendent of the colony and resident manager. While every colonist had freedom over his lot, Johnson felt that six acres to orchard, two to grapes and two to buildings and alfalfa-raising would be best.

The *San Juan Record*, on Sept. 4, 1958, printed this reminiscence of Ella and Anthony Landis, whose family moved to Orange Vale in 1889:

> In 1889 we moved to Orangevale where our father built the house in which we still live at 9001 Central Avenue. There were only three other families in Orangevale at that time. You had to be careful not to get off the trail to Fair Oaks or you could get lost in all the trees and hills.
>
> Orangevale was originally part of the San Juan Spanish land grant, but on December 14, 1844, J. P. Dedmond filed on the land. The Mexican government gave this land away so they could get people to pay taxes. Dedmond later sold to Hiram Grimes who in turn sold to a Mr. (Lansford W.) Hastings, and finally 4400 acres were sold at $6 per acre to Mr. Cardwell for whom Cardwell Colony was named.
>
> In the early 1880s Cardwell fenced and cleared the land. About 1885 he piled about 44,000 cords of wood on the bank of the American River and tried to bring a steamboat up to haul it away. However, this plan failed as a steamboat was unable to go under two bridges in Sacramento. So, some time later, the wood caught fire and burned
>
> Cardwell was a man of many interests and at one time he borrowed a sum of money from Mr. Ben Crocker. Later Crocker foreclosed on the mortgage and took 200 acres from the land east of Orangevale. So we bought that 200 acres from the Crocker Estate on September 21, 1901, and named it San (sic) Juanita Colony. We later sold it but the name remained. There is now a Santa Juanita Avenue running through it.
>
> The area known as Cardwell Colony is located north of Orangevale and the only land which Cardwell did not sell to the Orangevale Company in 1887. Cardwell made money as was evidenced by a thousand dollar them (sic) which he drove around. He also built a three-story house in Sacramento, made a trip to Ireland ... and did a lot of mining. He ultimately lost all of his money, though, and died in a cabin on the American River where he was mining. In spite of the fact that he did have a family, no funeral was held. In fact the people who buried him just dug a hole in the ground and put him in it, even without a coffin.
>
> We remember the fall of 1887 and the winter of 1888 when 10,000 oranges were put in at $1 per tree on the Orange Ranch here. They were destroyed by a freeze a short time later.

By 1890, 2,300 acres were fenced in and by 1894, 500 acres planted in oranges. The first crop was harvested in 1895. The colony grew slowly and in 1896 the Orange Vale Colonization Company was dissolved with all unsold land divided among the stockholders. Property owners were able to dispose of their lands as they saw fit. Some owners had a real estate firm publish a pamphlet expounding the marvels of the Orange Vale area, portraying the mild climate as even better than that of the Mediterranean Riviera.

The depression of the 1890s made all this publicity useless; few people came to Orange Vale to settle. But the area became an important producer of oranges. By 1913 there were more than 2,000 acres planted in orange trees.

The cold weather of December 1932, with a thermometer reading of 17 degrees, brought disaster to Orange Vale. Most of the trees were killed. In 1935 there remained only 879 acres of trees, and by 1940 this number was down to 473. Today most of the trees which helped Orange Vale prosper have been pulled out. The land they grew on has been subdivided even further to provide more housing for Sacramento's ever expanding population.

Fair Oaks

Fair Oaks was the second major land colony to be established on the San Juan grant. Much publicity had circulated in the Eastern states concerning the citrus colonies in California. Seeing this as a chance to sell their readers on the idea of a fruit colony, the Howard & Wilson Publishing Company of Chicago, publishers of Farm, Field and Fireside, sent a representative to the area to select a site. The oak trees along the American River, with Spanish moss hanging from their limbs, reminded the company's representative of Fair Oaks, Virginia, so he gave that name to the site.

The publishing company purchased 9,000 acres in March 1895, and began preparations to settle it. Given the name Sunset Colony, the land was divided into two parts: Fair

Fair Oaks was one of several land colonies established on the 20,000 acre San Juan grant in the late 1800s. Laid out as a community of small citrus, olive, and almond orchards, it was anchored by the store on the left, San Juan Hall on the right, and the school, from which this photo was taken.

Oaks and Olive Park. Five, ten and twenty acre lots could be bought for $100 to $120 per acre, with an additional $10 surcharge to construct an electric railroad linking the community to Sacramento.

The advertising statement pamphlet stated:

> Life is precious; why court pneumonia, consumption and death in this climate of the East Coast when, at a moderate cost, you can secure an ideal home and a sure income in Fair Oaks.

Fair Oaks' first settlers arrived in November of 1895. Also that month, an excursion train from Chicago brought 106 people to the colony, with the purpose of enticing people to buy land. Reports of the visit were published in the *Farm, Field and Fireside*:

> If the dispatches from Chicago report truly, while we are enjoying these luxuries of California climate, you unfortunates at Chicago are wrestling with a foot of snow with your railroads and street cars blocked, telegraph wires torn down, and enjoying the exuberant exercise of shoveling snow while sadly eyeing the rapidly depleting coal bins.

Excursionists were presented with handsome blue, white and gold satin badges on which the following verse was printed:

> Ah who would not live beyond the reach
>   of the snows,
> 'Mid the fragrance of orange, lemon
>   and rose,
> With the almond and olive and vine on
>   the Lea,
> In the summerland breeze late kissed by
>   the sea,
> Where all of nature's bounties are fairest
>   and free?

Miss Ella Landis and her brother Anthony remembered the excursion that came to town. In an interview that appeared in the *San Juan Record* on September 4, 1958 they said:

> We well remember the first excursion which came to Fair Oaks on November 14, 1895. Those people were first shown the heavily wooded area in Fair Oaks. Then, to show them what the country would look like under cultivation, they were brought to Orangevale, which had about a 10-year head start. Anthony was on the school playground during recess when they went by in a four-horse tallyho. The *Farm, Field and Fireside* publications which sponsored the excursion used a 136-year old Indian who lived in Fair Oaks as an example of long lives people would live who moved there. He was billed as the oldest man in the world and whether he was really 136 years old or not, we don't know, but he was pretty old …

"Bonny Fair Oaks, the gem of California," was plagued by difficulties during its early years. Water had to be hauled from the American River in barrels until July, 1896 when pipe was laid down in the town's main street. Unfortunately, it was a shoddy construction job and the pipe leaked profusely, the water supply remained inadequate. The electric railroad was never built, leaving the town isolated from Sacramento. The disgruntled residents held a meeting in the spring of 1898 to plan ways to force the publishing company to live up to its promises. The company, however, had transferred its title to a creditor, thereby escaping legal action. The colony was then taken over by the Fair Oaks Development Company.

By 1900 Fair Oaks had developed into a prosperous community. About 2,200 acres had been sold and 1,200 acres were planted in lemons, oranges, olives and almonds. The value of land had risen to $250 an acre. A bridge built across the American River eliminated the community's isolation. In 1900 about 300 people lived in the area.

Immer O. Rice had reminiscences of what Fair Oaks was like when he arrived in August 1906:

> The orchards were in full production, and the packing house was built that year. The Olive Mill was just a small wooden building at the same place where the concrete building is now. There were 7 houses between San Juan Avenue and the Twelfth Street Bridge to which a long wooden trestle was the approach. A small steel bridge, a lot lower than the present bridge, was the one across the American River here and was taken out by the flood of 1907 or 1908 in March ... There were many Hindus here at that time ... There were also a number of Japanese who worked in the fruit.

Fair Oaks' citrus orchards suffered the same fate as Orangevale's in the freeze of December 1932. The community grew very slowly until the boom years following World War II.

Carmichael

The third land colony to be promoted in this area was the Carmichael Colony, established by D. W. Carmichael in 1909. Carmichael purchased the western 2,000 acres of the San Juan grant, east of the present Manzanita Avenue, paying $75 an acre. When Rancho del Paso was sold and parceled in 1910 and 1911, he added 1,000 acres of the rancho to his land. Carmichael Colony was patterned after the already established colonies of Fair Oaks and Orangevale. The following promotional article appeared in *Sunset* magazine on May 1911:

> Carmichael Colony is advantageously situated in the shelter of the rolling foothills, secure from frosts; and the climate conditions peculiar to this section, combined with the extreme fertility of the soil, favor a citrus crop two months in advance of any other section of the United States.
>
> The weather bureau's report for the past thirty two years on localities visited by frost has excluded this section. Fair Oaks and Orangevale, our sister colonies, have shared with us in this report.
>
> Fortunes have been made and are being made here in the culture of citrus fruits, and aside from it being a remunerative industry it gives ample time for the owner to enjoy life in other pursuits. The [river and] woods hereabouts are stocked with trout for rod and ducks for gun. The climate insures the maximum of health-giving qualities and the temperature allows outdoor sleeping every night of the year.
>
> The possibilities are too many to enumerate here and we will ask that you write us for further details if interested, which we are sure you will be by this time. Now just a little in facts and figures: $750 will plant and take care of ten acres of oranges the first year. $100 will take care of the second year and the third year will pay all expenses of planting and care. The fourth year will realize you a substantial profit and from this time on the actual value of this ten acres will be approximately $10,000 and it will increase in value.
>
> Fruit companies here wish to foster the fruitgrowing industry and will gladly furnish trees for a small amount down, without interest, taking payment for the same when the trees bear fruit. To the man of moderate means this should prove interesting as there is nothing more profitable in land than a tract in Carmichael Colony.

Not a single Orange, Lemon or Pomeloe grown in Carmichael Colony lost its sweetness, color or exquisite flavor because of an unexpected and unusual visit of the Frost King to

California

D. W. CARMICHAEL
of Sacramento
Founder of Carmichael Colony

¶ Not a penny's worth of damage was done to the beautiful semi-tropical gardens of this magnificent, prosperous and productive section of the Sacramento Valley. Carmichael Colony is so located that its crops are sure and the quality of its products are unsurpassed.

Nothing in the way of a freak Winter ever occurred here to cause the settlers on **Carmichael Colony** a single hour of worry or disappointment. **Carmichael Colony** is absolutely beyond experiment as a place on which to build a home and achieve independence and contentment. Others have done it; others are doing it; why not you?

Land in **Carmichael Colony** will be sold on easy terms. A perpetual water right goes with every purchase. We help you to succeed and we locate you amid the best neighbors in the world who will also take an interest in your success.

We guarantee every inch of land to which we give you title. We place you in a neighborhood on the edge of Sacramento City, where the water is excellent, the roads are modern, schools are the best, churches are available and the environment is first-class in every particular. Cut out the attached coupon and mail it to-day. We will be pleased to send you a beautiful illustrated booklet on **Carmichael Colony** and give all information regarding this attractive and productive settlement in the Heart of California.

THE CARMICHAEL COLONY

SACRAMENTO CALIFORNIA

CARMICHAEL COMPANY
SACRAMENTO, CAL.

I am interested in your Colony. Forward literature and information.

Name ....

Address ....

State ....

*Carmichael Colony was
established by D. W.
Carmichael in 1909.
Ten acre lots sold
for $2,000.*

A 10-acre tract facing a forty-foot avenue and piped for water costs $2,000. Pay the price of $200 down and the remainder at the rate of $10 a month with six percent interest. Come and settle on the land and in a year's time it will pay for itself. For further particulars write the Carmichael Co, 800 J Street, Sacramento, Cal.

Harold J. Dewey's grandfather, Jacob Heintz, came to the area in 1890. An interview with Dewey appeared in the November 6, 1958 edition of the *San Juan Record*:

My father and grandfather farmed Carmichael Colony (then the Cox and Clark grant) together for years until 1900. They also farmed one section of land where Carmichael Park now is. Altogether they had 4,400 acres leased on a share basis with one-fourth of their earnings going to Cox and Clark and to the Haggin Grant (Carmichael Colony land). In those days bills were paid only once a year — after harvest. Farmers would simply charge their things all year long. And, incidentally, there were no interest charges. However, when one did pay his yearly bill, the creditor's policy was to take him out for a glass of whiskey at the nearest saloon. Even a non-drinking man had to engage in this custom as a friendly gesture.

It was a 2½-hour trip to Sacramento with only four houses between our place and town. In the very early days, that's where we had to get our paper and mail.

There was one year when our crop produced 5,400 sacks of wheat. It sold at 98 cents per 100 pounds.

In 1900 Cox and Clark sold all their land to Dan Carmichael, who started colonization so that served as one reason why my parents left their Palm Avenue home and moved to the Fair Oaks residence.

I also remember way back when a lot of orchards were being planted. There wasn't an hour would pass that you couldn't hear someone blasting holes for trees. In 1912 my father planted our first orchard, blasting and planting 27 acres of almonds. We now have 110 acres.

At the present time, our farm is the only one I know in this area which is still self-supporting — it supports two families.

Unfortunately for Carmichael, the popularity of fruit colonies passed, and the town developed very slowly. It was not until after WW II that Carmichael experienced rapid growth in population, with a 72,000 zip code total in 2005.

Folsom Prison

Bancroft, in his chronicles of early California, makes it clear that the seriousness and frequency of crime kept pace with the population explosion occasioned by the discovery of gold. As early as 1851 Governor Burnett was recommending the death penalty for grand larceny and robbery because the State simply lacked a place to hold convicted offenders.

San Quentin was the State's only prison until Folsom Prison was opened in 1880. Land for the site had been deeded to the State 10 years earlier by the Natoma Water and Mining Company in exchange for convict labor to build the company dam and canal at Folsom.

The cell-blocks were built of granite quarried on the spot and are still in use 100 years later. The original cell-blocks contained 324 cells. They were arranged in two tiers, along either side of a central aisle. Partitions between cells were 12 inches thick, and floors and ceilings were 10 inches thick. The door was solid iron with a 10 by 3 inch opening cut into the face for ventilation and observation. Doors were secured to the granite by three heavy strap-hinges and locked with a huge padlock.

Convicts are marched past the chapel in Folsom Prison, a different kind of colony. The prison was built on Natoma Water and Mining Company land deeded to the State in exchange for convict labor to build the dam and canal that provided water power to operate the nearby Folsom Power House.

Each cell was built to accommodate two prisoners. Furniture consisted of two each of wooden bunks, straw mattresses, pillows, blankets and buckets — one for drinking and the other for toilet facilities. Oil lamps served as both light and heat until electricity was brought to the prison in 1891.

A third cell-block was authorized in 1891, and in 1930 an additional 300 cells were constructed. In 1935 another 500 were built. A major new unit was completed in 1986, providing space for 3,000 new beds. But in 2005 the population had risen to 7,500, and there were again complaints of dangerous overcrowding.

Settlement East Of Sacramento

Communities between Sacramento and Folsom remained separate and distinct settlements, surrounded by open farmlands, until the WW II era. With the increase in population generated by the war, not only did east county communities grow in size, but the area between them and Sacramento gradually filled in.

River Park

One of the first of these new areas to be developed was River Park. This subdivision is well named, for not only is it bordered on the north and east by a bend in the American River, areas of it had been part of the river itself at one time. In 1943 when John Sandburg and Louis Carlson bought the land, they found there was no clear title to it because the river had once flowed thorough it. Over the years the river gradually shifted northward and eastward, squaring off the boundaries of the present-day subdivision. Since the river was considered navigable, it was under federal control, and Sandburg had to travel to Washington, D. C. to convince authorities to relinquish control over the old river bed. The State of California entered the conflict and claimed that the old river bottom was clearly State land. Sandburg and Carlson brought suit against the State for title to the land and won.

For several years during WW II the River Park area was farmed; tomatoes, alfalfa, spinach and peaches were principal crops. After the war Sacramento began to feel the pressure of population growth, and the area was annexed to the city, moving Sacramento's boundaries eastward. The real estate firm of Jones, Brand and Hullin, Inc. acquired the property and began plans to subdivide. The first map was filed in August, 1945 and construction started shortly after. Seventy-five acres were added to the tract in 1953 with the acquisition of the Elvas Farms area between 30th Street and River Park. With the coming of Sacramento State College (later California State University, Sacramento) in 1953, River Park began to boom. By 1959 its population was over 3,500.

Rancho Cordova

Rancho Cordova is another area where farmland was subdivided for residences after WW II. Historically, the area was known as Mills and was a center for fruit and hop production. It was incorporated in 2003 with these boundaries: American River on the north, Highway 16 (less airport) on the south, Hazel Avenue on the east and Bradshaw Road on the west.

In 1950, Roland Federspiel of Colonial Grape Products, faced with the rising costs of grape production, decided to subdivide his vineyard land. Mather Air Force Base was growing and the Aerojet General Corp. was planning to locate east of Sacramento on Natomas Company land. Federspiel was banking on the possibility that the employees of these companies would want to live near their work. As a test, six duplexes and eight homes were built on Alicante way in 1951 and were immediately occupied by Mather and Aerojet employees and families. In 1953 the subdivision got Federal Housing Authority approval. Federspiel formed the Rancho Cordova Corporation (named for Cordova Vineyards, predecessor to Colonial Grape Products) which included himself, his cousin Robert E. Hatch, a San Francisco attorney, and Alan T. Olson, owner of Brighton Sand and Gravel Company.

In the summer of 1953 the Jacobsen Construction Company started building homes on Zinfandel Drive. A grand opening of the subdivision in November featured master of ceremonies Art Linkletter, a radio personality and president of an electric company that produced some of the equipment installed in the homes. The corporation continued to build and, as it expanded, it named streets after different varieties of grapes that were grown in the area. Federspiel set a successful example and many other landowners began selling their land to subdivision developers to offset increased taxes and assessments.

As the old Mills area became suburbanized, social and civic needs of the community had to be met. Schools, parks, shopping centers, a postal system, a modern fire department and improved roads were established. The growth rate of Rancho Cordova has been rapid. In 1960 there were 4,080 dwellings, but by 1965 this rose to 7,855. In 1960 the population was 12,660 and by 1965 it had increased to 28,500. By 1968 the population was 38,000. Population was 55,000 in 2005.

College Greens

College Greens is another major area of development annexed to the eastern part of Sacramento. It is bounded on the west by the Southern Pacific Railroad; on the north by H Street and the American River; on the east by Watt Avenue, Manlove Road and the Elk Grove-Florin Road extension, and on the south by Fruitridge Road. The area north of Folsom Boulevard has newer residential units, while the area to the south is essentially industrial, mixed with pre-war housing.

Campus Commons

The West Arden Area is the land between Arden Way on the north, Watt Avenue on the east, and the American River to the south and west. When the 660-acre Campus Commons area was annexed in 1965 it was agricultural, with open land free of urban development. It was the first proposal approved by the City Planning Commission under the Planned Unit Development concept. The 129-acre East Ranch Planned Unit Development was acquired in 1967. The area had 571 homes by 1990, according to Campus Commons officials.

Salmon runs packed the river upstream as far as Salmon Falls at the upper end of present-day Folsom Reservoir. The fish were a staple of the Nisenan diet.

Chapter 10

The River's Fishery

You ask what it's like to catch a steelhead. It's almost mystical. The take can be subtle, but what happens afterward is always explosive. It's like sticking your finger in a light socket. If your line is too heavy, it'll avoid it. If the line is too light, it will break it. You may have to play it for 15 minutes or more. If you catch one, you won't forget it."

— Jim Jones, Past President, Save the American River Association
— and avid steelhead fisherman

Throughout its history, the American River has been rich in wildlife, and in many ways it still is. Lampreys, sturgeon, steelhead trout, Sacramento pikeminnow (formerly squawfish), western suckers, and especially the Chinook or king salmon were among the native species that thrived in the river before the gold rush.

In the 1870s, government fish culturists introduced American shad and striped bass. These fish have made the American River a permanent home. In the quiet backwaters along the river, introduced warm water fish such as bluegill, crappie, and largemouth and smallmouth bass add to the variety of fish life. Several species are anadromous, growing in size in the ocean, and returning to fresh water to spawn. These include the Chinook salmon, steelhead trout, lamprey, American shad, and striped bass. The lower American River now has approximately 43 species of native and introduced fish.

Of all the species, salmon have been the most important since Indian days. This fish was a regular food of the Nisenan Indians for whom the beginning of the large salmon run in the fall was a time of celebration. The salmon begin their spawning run in late September. Female salmon lay eggs in gravel nests called *redds* that they make in the river. Male salmon swim over the eggs and fertilize them. The females then cover the eggs with rocks, and make more nests downstream until they are spent. The run peaks in November and then tapers off through January. Nisenan collected the fish during this migration, then dried and stored the meat for year-round use.

Prior to the establishment of dams on the American River, at least 125 miles of stream, including the South, North, and Middle forks, were available to spawning salmon. Estimates are that the American River may have supported salmon runs exceeding 130,000 fish annually before the river system was altered.

Hydraulic mining debris, pollution, and other artificial barriers drastically reduced the runs so that between 1944 and 1955 the average number of salmon spawning below

Folsom was estimated to be 26,500 fish. Of these spawners, 73 percent used the gravel beds between the Folsom and Nimbus Dam sites. Recent counts range from a low of 11,000 total salmon in the river in the winter of 1990-'91, to a high of 117,000 in the winter of 1987-'88.

Folsom Dam

When Folsom Dam was constructed, the U.S. Bureau of Reclamation built the Nimbus Fish Hatchery to replace lost spawning beds. The California Department of Fish and Game operates the hatchery. The Bureau pays the operational costs.

A portion of the salmon population still spawns naturally in the river's gravel riffles, from the vicinity of the Watt Avenue Bridge upstream to the Nimbus Hatchery fish racks. Survival of eggs and young fish varies, however due to the river's temperature and flow being affected by the operation of the dam. Spawning beds and nursery areas may alternate between being deeply flooded and left high and dry at crucial times.

Another problem is that heavy spring and summer releases from Folsom Lake for flood control and agricultural use often leave only a low pool of sun-warmed lake water from which to supply flows for the fall salmon run. When water temperatures are too high, many fish retain their eggs. Eggs that are laid in the gravel do not hatch and the sur-

Watching the salmon jump up the fish ladder into Nimbus Hatchery is a popular fall pastime. The U. S. Bureau of Reclamation built the hatchery as mitigation for the natural salmon runs cut off by Nimbus and Folsom dams.

Nimbus hatchery, operated by the California Department of Fish and Game, lies just below Nimbus Dam. A screen across the river directs the fish into the ladder leading to the hatchery, where the fish are artificially spawned.

Mercury Problem Cited

The California Environmental Protection Agency cautioned consumers in 2004 of possible health hazards from eating too much fish from Lake Natoma and the Lower American River. The threat stems from toxic mercury that was used to extract gold in the mining process long ago having built up in the food chain. Cited fish included channel catfish, all bass, white catfish, pikeminnow, sucker, bluegill, and sunfish. The agency urged limiting consumption to none at all for channel catfish by women of childbearing age and children age 17 and younger, to one meal a month by others for other fish. Details are available at the agency's website www.oehha.ca.gov/fish/hg/index.html.

vival of hatched fish decreases. The warm water also affects hatching and survival in the Nimbus hatchery into which the remainder of the run is diverted by the fish rack and ladder. Recently, some structural dam modifications, and operational modifications, have been made to lessen this problem.

So, for the highest returns of adults, several things have to happen together: 1. The river needs adequate cool water conditions for the adults to spawn in; 2. High spring flows for the downstream migration of their "smolts" or small fry; 3. Good food levels and proper temperatures in the ocean for two to three years; and 4. Sufficient cool water again for the return of the adults.

At the hatchery, the fish are artificially spawned, the eggs hatched in trays, and the young reared in concrete ponds until they are ready for release. The fish leaping up the ladder draw thousands of spectators. The hatchery, with the assistance of the Effie Yeaw Nature Center, developed a popular interpretive program there.

The hatchery has a capacity of 12 million eggs. Its production is an important contribution to the river's sport fishery and to the much larger ocean commercial and sport fishery. The Department of Fish and Game estimates that in a normal water year, one out of every six Chinook salmon caught along the California coast originates in the American River. The Chinook salmon ranges in weight between 15 and 45 pounds in the American River. Fish weighing more than 100 pounds have been caught in Alaskan waters.

Some steelhead trout also spawn naturally in the river. They are also affected by the variation in flows and temperatures. As a result, in recent years, Nimbus hatchery production has provided most of the fishery. Steelhead begin their migration from the ocean in the fall and winter and continue through March. Unlike salmon, they do not necessarily die after spawning. The hatchery returns spawned-out fish to the river. Some steelhead may return from the ocean for two or even three spawning runs. A sea-run rainbow trout, steelhead may reach 20 pounds in weight, but usually range between five and 10 pounds for adult winter-run fish. It is considered one of the finest of all game fish.

Recreational Fishery

Winter steelhead fishing in the American and similar northern California streams has been a popular sport for many years. There is no ocean fishery and no commercial take.

During late spring and early summer, the run of American shad enters the river on a spawning migration. Unlike salmon and steelhead, shad do not construct redds or nests, but spawn in open water.

Striped bass also frequent the river in spring and summer, feeding extensively on crayfish and lamprey young, but also on salmon and steelhead. From a recreational point of view, however, when the runs of shad and striped bass are added to those of salmon and steelhead, the result is an almost year-round sport fishery on the lower American. The river's fisheries are also a significant contributor to the region's economy.

Chapter 11

The American River Parkway

When I first moved here there was still gravel mining going on in the Parkway, and there were a lot of other activities going on as well. Because of that (1972) bond effort and because of the efforts of countless citizens, the Parkway was saved for future generations...
— Sacramento County Supervisor Illa Collin, 2003

The American River Parkway, now ranked among Sacramento's finest resources, stretches 31 1/2 miles from the confluence of the American and Sacramento Rivers to Beal's Point in Folsom Lake State Recreation Area. It preserves a precious open space greenbelt through a largely metropolitan area with a population of more than 1.3 million people. It serves as habitat for a great assortment of wildlife and a source of recreational opportunities for people with many interests — fishing, boating, rafting, bicycling, picnicking, bird watching, nature study, lying on the beach. The creation of the Parkway is a remarkable story that crowns the history of the Lower American River.

Early Proposals

Early in the 20th century the concept of an American River Parkway was already taking shape. In 1915, John Nolen, a Sacramento city planner, submitted to the City Commissioners of Sacramento the results of a study done under the direction of the Board of Park Directors. The study, which was to project a city plan that would meet the future needs of the capital, showed an extensive park system that included a continuous park area along the American River. A map reflecting this early plan referred to this area as the "American River Parkway." Though Nolen's plan is not the specific plan on which the present parkway is based, his is the first known reference to the concept of an American River Parkway.

Frederick Law Olmsted Jr

More than a decade later, in 1929, after the passage of the first state park bond act, Frederick Law Olmsted Jr., son of the renowned landscape architect and city planner who designed New York's Central park, surveyed the entire state for its park and recreation potentials. In the Sacramento area, Olmsted was particularly attracted to the scenic views from the levee roads and urged that construction along these roads be regulated. He envisioned these roads as attractive routes within the parkway plan that he proposed for the Sacramento River and its tributaries. He also recommended cooperative efforts among the agencies with jurisdiction over the various aspects of the river area — flood control, conservation and use of water, highway transportation and preservation and use of scenic and recreational areas.

In 1947, Olmsted updated his plan, and included a more complete proposal for parkway development in the Sacramento area. Olmsted's proposal emphasized development of recreational facilities, including public parking, picnic sites and possible docks for pleasure craft, with development adjacent to the proposed parkway through local planning and zoning.

As Sacramento continued to grow through the first decades of the 20th century, the river flood plan was held in private ownership and seasonal floods kept commercial development out of the river area. Some land along the river was farmed while sand and gravel operations occupied other portions of the flood plain. Still, much of the natural vegetation and wildlife habitat was preserved, attracting people who came to enjoy the river and its groves of oaks and cottonwoods. Access was limited, however, so that interest in pursuing a public parkway grew.

Much of the river was still lined with dense riparian habitat at the beginning of the Twentieth Century.

First Acquisitions Along River

Early in 1949, the River Beautification Committee, consisting of representatives of the city and county government and the Chamber of Commerce, was created. The commission's purpose was to outline tentative plans for a program designed to beautify and develop recreational areas on the American River, as well as prepare maps of the territory between Sacramento and Folsom. The State Park Commission had set aside a $200,000 fund to acquire land along the Sacramento and American Rivers for parks if local organizations could provide matching money or potential park land. With two years to take advantage of these state funds, the City of Sacramento soon became active in park acquisitions.

In September, 1950, the City Council voted unanimously to acquire 82 acres of land on the south bank of the river, one mile below the H Street Bridge, for "park, general recreational and swimming purposes" in the River Park neighborhood. Seventy-five acres of land were donated by John Sandburg and Louis D. Carlson, while seven acres were purchased by the city for $200,000. Adjacent to Paradise Beach, the park was named after Glenn Hall, an engineer of Sacramento City who strongly espoused the 1947 Olmsted proposal.

The 1950s also saw a surge in urban development expanding away from the heart of the City of Sacramento and to land bordering the river. Then in 1955, completion of Folsom and Nimbus Dams controlled the flood danger and opened the river area to commercial and housing development. The time to take aggressive action on the parkway concept had come.

Parkway Idea Adopted

In March 1959 the Sacramento County Board of Supervisors adopted an ordinance establishing a County Department of Parks and Recreation and development of the park system began. The first park development director, William B. Pond, a seasoned Pacific Northwest parks and recreation manager, was hired in 1959. He soon discovered there was strong public support for a plan to open up recreational opportunities along the lower American River. He later was to recall:

"The horsemen dreamed of a capital-to-capital trail — Sacramento to Carson City. The bicyclists wanted a paved path from the confluence to Nimbus Dam, hikers wanted the same, and the Audubon Society and the environmentalists wanted access to all of the natural elements, and the fishermen and canoeists and kayakers wanted access to the river."

The supervisors liked the idea of a master plan for the 23 miles of river front from Nimbus Dam to the confluence of the Sacramento River. (The 8½ miles of parkway from Nimbus Dam to Folsom Lake is federal Bureau of Reclamation land managed by the State Parks Department.) Land acquisition began. But initial purchases were expensive and progress was slow. With most of the river still inaccessible to the public, many residents — especially newcomers — did not realize its recreational potential. When resistance to further county spending developed, the project lagged.

The Community Organizes

In February, 1961 the County Planning Commission approved plans for a subdivision within 125 feet of the river. This was the act that rallied parkway forces. Within a few days a small group of civic leaders and representatives of conservation and youth groups met to lay the groundwork for the Save the American River Association (SARA). Among these leaders were Effie Yeaw and Jim Mullaney. (Today a nature center in the Parkway recognizes Effie Yeaw's role, while an oak grove on the river's edge at Rossmoor Bar honors Jim Mullaney.)

A July day in the early '30s at a beach and giant slide near the H Street Bridge in today's River Park.

SARA speakers covered the community, recruited members, distributed pamphlets and prepared a film *Operation STAR — Save the American River*. Their enthusiasm and hard work rallied the support necessary to convince the supervisors that the community was behind the preservation of the river and its bordering wild lands. In January, 1962 the board officially adopted the Parkway plan and committed more funds for acquisition.

Under the direction of parks director Bill Pond, the county acquired rights to land from many sources. Several private land owners turned down offers from developers and sold to the county at reasonable prices; others granted easements. More funds came from the California Wildlife Conservation Board, a state agency, and the Urban Renewal Administration, a federal agency. SARA, too, raised funds by selling "Elbow Room," square yards of land to which the buyer received a "certificate of ownership;" the county received title. This open space on the south bank in Carmichael is now known as SARA Park.

First Parkway Acquisitions

By 1965 the county had acquired three large parcels along the Parkway, making purchases as land became available. Goethe Park was acquired in stages between 1961 and 1964. Charles Mathias Goethe was a well-known Sacramento writer, naturalist and philanthropist. His family established a fund in his name for the purpose of land acquisition which made possible purchase of the wooded area on the south bank of the river.

Ancil Hoffman Park, originally a farming area known as San Juan Meadows, was acquired in 1961. The orchards and grazing land became a golf course and playing field, with the undisturbed northerly portion preserved for nature study. The park was named for County Supervisor Ancil Hoffman, who represented that district at the time. Hoffman was a rabid golfer in his earlier years. At one time he was the manager of Max Baer, Sacramento's only World Heavyweight Boxing Champion.

Ancil Hoffman Park is the home of the Effie Yeaw Nature Center, which since its founding in 1976 has drawn thousands of visitors young and old to its natural history, cultural history and environmental programs keyed to local school science curricula. Supported by volunteers aged from 14 to 80, the county facility provides hands-on exhibits, including a Nisenan Maidu Indian village and tours of the 71-acre nature area with its deer, turkeys and many other wildlife species.

Discovery Park, at the confluence with the Sacramento River, was acquired in 1961-

64. This park unit is noted for its boat launching facilities and fishing access. The south bank of the river mouth is known as Tiscornia Park. A popular sandy beach, it honors Captain Edward R. Tiscornia, a U.S. marine killed in WWII.

When a $12.6 million bond issue was overwhelming approved by voters in 1972, land acquisition accelerated. Approximately 80 percent of the money was to be used for acquisition and development within the Parkway. Among the development projects were a bicycle trail, equestrian and hiking trail bridge across the river, and the Effie Yeaw Nature Center in Ancil Hoffman Park.

In 1974 with funds from the bond issue, Sacramento County acquired the 269-acre Arden Sand and Gravel property on the north side of the river from owner Frank Erickson. This site was known as Arden Bar, later renamed the William B. Pond Recreation Area in honor of the first county parks director, who came to be recognized as "Father of the American River Parkway" for his leadership in carrying out the first parkway plan.

The Board of Supervisors also agreed to purchase a 42-acre parcel at the upper end of the William B. Pond Recreation Area, linking two portions of the bicycle trail. When the Jedediah Smith Memorial Bridge was opened in 1980, it allowed the trail to extend the full length of the Parkway. Later this bridge was dedicated to Harold Richey, avid cyclist and bike trail advocate. (Ch. 5).

Throughout the long process of land acquisition, the Natomas Company was noted for its support and cooperation. As a major landowner along the river, the company played an important role in the creation of the American River Parkway. Dante Lembi, a senior company official, was a major force in getting the Parkway established.

Parkway Plan

The Parkway became part of the County's General Plan in 1962, and by 1968 it had been expanded to include the location of natural and recreational areas, access points, and proposed development.

After further study and hearings, a new plan was adopted in 1978. Environmental groups vigorously advocated preservation of the natural character of the river corridor, and the new plan ruled out development of recreation facilities that were not river-related. There would be no more golf courses, and tennis courts and baseball diamonds would go elsewhere. The plan called for review or revision every five years. Community environmentalists let by SARA, "blew the whistle" on proposals for development or change along the river.

Land within the Parkway falls under several political jurisdictions. Several units, including Discovery Park and Paradise Beach, are within the City of Sacramento. Some lands are held by Scout and Campfire organizations. As mentioned, the state manages the land above Nimbus Dam and holds title to the flood plain along the Cal Expo site.

Cal Expo — Bushy Lake

The state acquired 1,000 acres for the Cal Expo site in 1950 from Mr. and Mrs. Robert Swanston, Sr. and Jr. for $8.5 million. In 1958 the legislature appropriated $7.5 million and authorized a $13 million revenue bond issue for construction. The project opened in 1968.

In 1973 Governor Ronald Reagan shifted operation of Cal Expo from the Department of General Services to the State Park System. Department director William Penn Mott, Jr. planned to develop the unused portion of the exposition site into an area for year-round recreation.

Eppie's Great Race competitors run, paddle and bicycle more than 37 miles along American River Parkway in what is billed as world's oldest triathlon. Restaurateur Eppie Johnson began the charity event in 1974.

Aroused by this proposal, supporters of a natural parkway pushed for protection of the area. As a result, the Bushy Lake Preservation Act, authored by Assemblyman Eugene Gualco, D-Sacramento, was approved by the Legislature in 1976. Concern over Cal Expo's use of the land prompted the county, with the help of Assemblymen Lloyd Connelly, D-Sacramento, and Phil Isenberg, D-Sacramento, to negotiate a seven-year lease agreement with the Cal Expo Board of Directors. The lease called for the county to assume management responsibility during this period. A management plan that would preserve the area as riparian wetlands and wildlife habitat was adopted by the county in 1988.

But the issue flared five years later when it was learned that Cal Expo planned a 40-acre parking facility in the parkway near Bushy Lake, touching off strong opposition from environmental groups. The site would be used to handle 5,000 cars in overflow traffic during the State Fair and other events during the year. The proposal was backed by state legislation, but after a year-long fight led by the Save The American River Association, the measure was dropped, thereby protecting important parkway wildlife habitat.

Continuing the effort to coordinate management among agencies, in 1990 Assemblyman Connelly proposed legislation to place the Bureau of Reclamation land managed by State Parks upriver between Nimbus and Folsom Dams under the same administration and management policies as the rest of the parkway. His bill was vetoed by Governor Deukmejian at the request of State Parks, apparently on the grounds that it might set a statewide precedent for local control of state park lands.

The 8½ miles of the parkway extending from Nimbus Dam to Beal's Point on Folsom Lake is increasingly popular with the extension of the bicycle-hiking-horseback riding trail to the south side of Lake Natoma in 1999-2001, thus encircling Lake Natoma. The lake also features swimming and picnicking and the California State University, Sacramento, Aquatic Center with classes and rentals of kayaks, canoes and other water craft.

Challenges.

After a lengthy career as Sacramento County Parks Director, Gene Andal would say in 2005 that next to the lack of adequate operational funding for parks, his biggest challenge was the issue of private development intruding on the parkway. He was referring to proposals to build large homes comprising as much as 10,000 square feet on parkway bluffs that offered panoramic views of the river and beyond. Beginning in the late 1980s, a dozen building proposals called for adding second levels, encroaching on cliff-edge erosion zones, or replacing one house with as many as three.

It was a case of private property rights vs. zoning laws. Parkway supporters pointed to a 1987 county zoning law calling on government to "insure that development with access within and adjacent to the American River Parkway is designed to reduce as much as possible visual intrusion into the parkway and to complement the naturalistic amenities of the parkway."

Too often, says Frank Cirill, president emeritus of the Save the American River Association, the Board of Supervisors has ignored that directive. Sensitive building proposals in the parkway corridor have often led to lengthy hearings, lawsuits and split decisions by the Board of Supervisors approving exemptions to zoning laws.

The importance of grassroots support for the parkway was underscored in the protracted struggle over the future of the prized Fair Oaks Bluff, one of the outstanding "viewscapes" in Sacramento County. The 4.5 acres of gently rolling grasslands and oaks atop the 140-foot high bluff offers public access to views of the Sierra, Mount Diablo and the winding

The Lower American River is a magnet for anglers pursuing Chinook Salmon, Steelhead, Striped Bass and shad. Salmon range from 15 to 45 pounds in weight.

Boat ramp project crews work near old Fair Oaks Bridge The span washed out twice and was rebuilt twice in early 1900s and now is limited to pedestrians, cyclists and equestrians.

American River. It had been earmarked for development until a citizens group started and coordinated by American River College teacher Tracy Martin Shearer, with the help of the Sacramento Valley Conservancy, raised over $1 million to acquire half the property and turn it over to the County in 2003 for inclusion in the American River Parkway. The Fair Oaks Recreation and Park District signed for a bank loan obtained by the citizens group on the remaining half as both groups had fundraising drives to secure the second half of the bluff.

In another example of the fight to block intruding developments, parkway activists joined county parks staff to head off potential construction on a broad, grassy area in Discovery Park. With funding by the Sacramento Downtown Rotary Club, scores of Boy Scouts and other volunteers planted 500 oaks, sycamores and other trees in an area that had stood sun-baked and unused in summer.

Future

Planning and development of the American River Parkway is a classic work in progress. As of 2005, two major parcels of land totaling 127 acres within the designated parkway were still in private ownership and slated for acquisition, but no funds were available for this purpose.

As with other regional parks in California, The American River Parkway is affected by state and county funding cuts as spending for law enforcement and health and welfare costs increased well into the new century. For instance, the Sacramento County general fund's net allocation for parks and open space fell 28.4 percent from $6.4 million in fiscal 1991-92 to $5 million in 2004-05. As a result, parks department staffing was cut by 43 percent to 75 employees, impacting law enforcement, maintenance and education services on the parkway. By 2005, a coalition of County parks supporters was planning a ballot measure calling for a new tax that would provide stable, long-term funding to maintain and improve county parks, including the parkway.

Such funding would help parks officials cope with law enforcement problems created by the community's burgeoning population and visitors from as far away as the Bay Area, drawn by the river's rafting and other recreational opportunities. The limited force of park rangers not only must investigate burglaries and robberies, they also issue thousands of citations annually for homeless camping, drug use, unleashed dogs, speeding on the bike trail, and under-age drinking. The last offense is especially prevalent during Memorial Day, July Fourth and Labor Day weekends as rafts laden with young people with ice chests float down the river. However, passage of a county transportation ballot measure in 2004 earmarked $1 million annually for increased bike trail ranger patrols and maintenance beginning in 2009.

Because of the parkway's natural beauty and prime recreational opportunities, it was apparent that its continuing health would require ongoing efforts of three grassroots non-profit organizations.

After rallying the community to get behind formation of the parkway in 1961, the Save the American River Association plays a vital "watchdog" role on behalf of preserving and protecting the parkway and Lower American River. SARA's stalwarts are usually the first to go to court, testify at hearings, and write letters to the editor to stop threats to the river and parkway.

The American River Natural History Association was formed in 1981 to support the Effie Yeaw Nature Center when it was scheduled for closure for lack of funding. In pursuing its mission to "bring people to nature and nature to people," it supports the nature center with such programs as hiring bus service to bring school children to the nature area for educational programs. Through volunteer efforts and fundraising, ARNHA pursues its educational efforts through publications such as this history, public forums, a quarterly journal-newsletter, interpretive kiosks on the parkway, exhibits, the annual Salmon Festival celebrating the return of the river's Chinook Salmon, and the Nature Bowl competition for school children.

The American River Parkway Foundation was formed in 1983 to raise funds to complete land acquisition of the Parkway. The Foundation also coordinates volunteer work to help preserve and restore the Parkway. It organizes two major events each year: the Great American River Cleanup and Down River Day, the latter, a major fundraiser. It initiated the Adopt-the-Parkway program, enlisting volunteers to care for the Parkway. In 2004 it broke ground for a visitor center at the William B. Pond Recreation Area.

The California Native Plant Society developed a presence on the parkway with establishment in 2001 of its "Weed Warriors" unit under the direction of Frank Wallace. In four years, the volunteer corps of mostly young people had removed invasive, non-native plants such as red sesbania, Spanish Broom and Pampas Grass that threatened to crowd out native vegetation on 600 acres of the parkway.

The American River Parkway has become more than a resource of local interest. Annual use of the Parkway exceeds the annual attendance level of every federal and state park in California except the Golden Gate National Recreational Area. The recreational values of the Lower American River have been determined to be of such significance that this portion of the river has been designated a "Recreational River" in both the federal and state Wild and Scenic Rivers systems, and the Parkway's trail system has been designated a National Recreational Trail.

On a river where gold was once the symbol of riches, now the flowing waters, the great variety of wildlife and the extraordinary opportunities for recreation give the Lower American a value beyond measure. May future chapters of the history of the river record continued preservation of this priceless resource.

The Parkway provides welcome tranquility in hectic urban lives.

Bibliography

American River Parkway General Review Program. Study Report I. September 14, 1973. Study Report II. October 15, 1973.

Aubury, Lewis. *Gold Dredging in California*. Sacramento, CA: State Mining Bureau, 1910.

Bancroft, Hubert Howe. *The History of California*. 7 Vols. San Francisco, CA: The History Company, 1884-1890.

Barber and Baker. *Sacramento Illustrated*. Sacramento, CA: Barber and Baker, 1855.

Basic Placer Mining. Special Publication 41, rev. from Mineral Information Services, 10:8. San Francisco, CA: California Division of Mines and Geology, 1957.

Bayley, Thomas S. "Reminiscences." *Golden Notes* (November 1967): 14:1-12.

Bryant, Edwin. *What I Saw in California*. Minneapolis, MN: Ross and Haines, 1961.

Buffum, Edward G. *Six Months in the Gold Mines*. Philadelphia, PA: 1850.

Calhoon, F. D. *California Gold and the Highgraders*. Sacramento, CA: CAL-CON Press, 1988.

Caughey, John W. *California: A Remarkable State's Life History*. Englewood Cliffs, NJ: Prentice-Hall, 1970.

Clark, William B. *Gold Districts of California*. Bulletin 193. San Francisco, CA: Division of Mines and Geology, 1963

Cooper, Erwin. *Aqueduct Empire*. Glendale, CA: Arthur H. Clark Co., 1968.

Daily Alta Californian. (San Francisco).

Davies, J. Kenneth. *Mormon Gold - The Story of California's Mormon Argonauts*. Salt Lake City, UT: Olympus Publishing Co., 1984.

De Voto, Bernard. *The Year of Decision, 1846*. 1942. Intro. Stephen E. Ambrose. Truman Talley Books. New York, NY: St. Martin's Press, 2000.

Dillinger, William C. *The Gold Discovery: James Marshall and the California Gold Rush*. Sacramento, CA: California Department of Parks and Recreation, 1990.

Emparen, Madie Brown. *The Vallejos of California*. San Francisco, CA: University of San Francisco, 1968.

Folsom Telegraph.

Gudde, Erwin G. *California Place Names*. Berkeley, CA: University of California Press, 1966

Hoover, Mildred Brook, Hero Eugene Rensch, and Mildred Rensch. *Historic Spots in California.* Stanford, CA: Stanford University Press, 1948.

Hutchings' California Magazine. II:5. (November 1857).

Jenkins, Olaf. *Geology of Placer Deposits.* Publication 34. San Francisco, CA: California Division of Mines and Geology, 1964.

Lewis, Oscar. *Sutter's Fort.* Englewood Cliffs, NJ: Prentice-Hall, 1966.

McGowan, Joseph A. *History of the Sacramento Valley.* 2 Vols. New York and West Palm Beach: Lewis Historical Publishing Co., 1961.

Neasham, V. Aubrey and James E. Henley. *The City of the Plain.* Sacramento, CA: Pioneer Foundation and Sacramento Historic Landmarks Commission, 1969.

Oakland Tribune.

Olmstead, Frederick Law. *California State Parks Survey.* Sacramento, CA: 1929.

Pacific Rural Press.

Paul, Rodman W. *California Gold.* Nebraska: University of Nebraska, 1965.

"Physical Development Elements of the Regional General Plan." Sacramento Regional Area Planning Commission (May 1971).

Plimpton, John. Unpublished papers, filed in "Black Binder #65," Archives of the California Department of Parks and Recreation, 1970.

Preuss, Charles. *Exploring with Fremont.* Norman, OK: University of Oklahoma Press, 1958

Rolle, Andrew E. *California: A History.* New York, NY: Thomas Y. Crowell, 1969.

Sacramento Bee.

Sacramento Bee. *Sacramento County and Its Resources.* Sacramento, CA: H.S. Crocker Co., 1895.

Sacramento City Directories. (Published under various titles and by different companies from 1850 to present).

Sacramento Union.

Savage, William S. *The Negro on the Mining Frontier.* Washington, D.C.: 1945.

Severson, Thor. *Sacramento, An Illustrated History: 1839-1874.* San Francisco, CA: California Historical Society, 1973.

Starr, Kevin. *Americans and the California Dream 1850-1915.* 1973. Reprint Edition. New York, NY: Oxford University Press, 1986.

Sutter, John A. *New Helvetia Diary.* San Francisco, CA: Society of California Pioneers, 1939.

Thompson, Thomas H. and Albert Augustus West. *History of Sacramento County.* Oakland, CA: Thompson and West, 1880.

Wagner, Jack R. *Gold Mines of California.* Berkeley, CA: Howell-North, 1986.

Index

Note:
- Page numbers in italics indicate illustrations.
- Page numbers followed by *(2)* or *(3)* indicate two or three separate discussions on the page.
- Page numbers followed by *cap* indicate captions.
- Page numbers followed by *map* indicate maps.
- Page numbers followed by *n* indicate footnotes.
- Page numbers followed by *q* indicate quotations.
- Page ranges linked by "/" indicate page ranges interrupted by full page illustrations.
- Page ranges linked by "---" indicate a number of separate discussions within the range.

Photo Credits

All illustrations are from the Sacramento Archives and Museum Collection Center, History and Science Division, Department of Parks and Community Serves, City of Sacramento, except the following:

Aerojet General, 85

Effie Yeaw Nature Center, Page 3

California Department of Parks & Recreation, Pages 21, 23, 28, 37

James Jones, Pages 4, 20

U.S. Bureau of Reclamation, Pages 73, 108, 109

Appendix

history map of the

Lower American River

historical time line

Lower American River

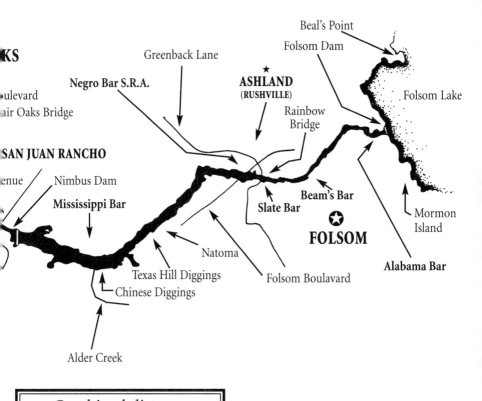

KS

ulevard
air Oaks Bridge

Negro Bar S.R.A.

Greenback Lane

ASHLAND
(RUSHVILLE) ★

Beal's Point

Folsom Dam

Folsom Lake

SAN JUAN RANCHO

enue

Nimbus Dam

Rainbow
Bridge

Mississippi Bar

Beam's Bar

Slate Bar

Mormon
Island

Natoma

⊛
FOLSOM

Texas Hill Diggings

Folsom Boulavard

Alabama Bar

Chinese Diggings

Alder Creek

Combined distance
Sacramento to Beal's Point:
31.5 miles

1945 River Park subdivision established

1950 Aerojet General plans $60 million rocket plant at Nimbus

1950 City buys land next to Paradise Beach for park

1955 Historic flood causes $150 million damage

1956 Folsom Dam completed

1959 William B Pond hired as first county parks director

1961 Save the American River Association founded

1961 Ancil Hoffman Park acquired

1961-64 Goethe Park, Discovery Park acquired

1972 Voters approve $12 6 million bond issue to expand parkway

1974 Arden Bar, later William B Pond Recreation Area, added to Parkway

1976 Effie Yeaw Nature Center dedicated

1976 Bushy Lake Preservation Act

1981 American River Natural History Association founded

1983 American River Parkway Foundation founded

1986 Record rains cause near flood

1989 Hodge decision's public trust issues

1995 Folsom Dam's broken spillway

2003 Fair Oaks Bluff preservation

2004 Folsom Dam raising authorized